Sales Analysis
Tool Kit

Your Guide to a Better Sales Team

By: Gary D. Seale

Thanks to the "Iron Men" in Austin Texas who are not concerned about speaking up to tell the truth, voice their opinions and share their experience.

Dan Forbes

Danny Smith

Scott Carley

Dale Miller

John Russell

Brian Henson

Joey McGirr

A special note of **Thanks to John Fincher** for his editing assistance and expertise.

Gary D. Seale The Trucon Consulting Group, LLC

Contact the Author: trucon@sbcglobal.net

IBSN: 9781707945665

Previous publications by Gary D. Seale: *Business Principles From Proverbs*

Forward

In our world of complexity and high-speed pursuit of our goals, it is common for a sales person, sales team or sales manager to get side tracked into a set of behaviors that do not produce the deep results we want. Owners often delegate the sales functions because it's not their area of expertise and they are legitimately busy with the other functions of the company.

However, if we do not pause and take time to analyze the people, target market, products, message, sales revenue and reputation (Among many other aspects of the company's environment) then we run the risk of heading blindly down the path of mediocrity and ultimately the demise of your dreams and livelihood.

The series of questionnaires were developed over decades of being involved in the sales world as a buyer, rookie salesperson, area sales manager, regional sales manager, product manager, international accounts manager, sales consultant and sales services provider.

The challenge is for you to take these questionnaires and step outside the inherent bias that exists around your own efforts. It will be important for you to be as objective as possible. Take time to mull over the questions, realizing that how you answer may well direct not only your future, but the future of the company.

Part of your analysis is to understand the people on your team as well as yourself. Be sure to take the personality tests and read the results to understand your strengths and inherent motivations. Discovering that you have a square peg in a round hole is much better now for both that person and the future of the company.

There are three training modules included in your analysis book. The Business to Business sales module is a concise 36 pages that helps a new person understand their job responsibilities and will serve as a refresher for the experienced individual.

The Sales Negotiation training module is an essential piece of information for the person who has the authority to conduct business for the company in the open marketplace. Both training modules have exercises included which will challenge you to think about the concepts and how they will be applied in your business.

You will also find included a step-by-step process of establishing a LinkedIn mining process that will allow you to obtain the names and contact information of key individuals in your target market. Trucon can assist with training or contract data mining services in this area.

A Proverb for Salespeople

12:14 "From the fruit of their lips people are filled with good things, and the work of their hands brings them reward."

Advance Reader's Recommendations

"Gary Seale has compiled a treasure trove of knowledge, experiences, insights, and sage advice that are useful in many situations and on many levels. Whether you are a business owner or executive taking an introspective look at your business, a sales manager wanting to hire or improve the effectiveness of your team, or a sales professional – new or experienced – wanting to "sharpen the saw", there I something here for you.

I highly recommend not only reading this, but keeping handy as a reference manual for running the sales side of your business."

Jeff Stec – President
Tylerica Marketing Systems, LLC

"As a leadership development coach to entrepreneurs and corporations, I am excited about resources to support the sales management team. This guide provides solid training and practical tools to coach a highly effective sales force. I can't wait to share this valuable resource with my clients that are ready to take their sales performance to the next level! "

Tammy McKinney, Maxwell Business and Life
Coach - Unlocking Your Best Life

"Gary Seale is right on target with so many things that it is great to know that he has put his approach to print. Now others can learn from his insights and wisdom."

John Russell – President
Russell Consulting Group

"Gary Seale not only knows how to develop and lead a sales team, he also knows how to capture the optimal processes involved and share them in a concise, understandable way so they can be implemented and measured. I highly recommend his new book, ***Sales Analysis Tool Kit.*** In fact, I like it so much that we are beginning to use it as a key aid in our sales program."

Roger L. Smith – President
Technical Specialties LLC
Guadalajara, Mexico

"Gary Seale's marketing and sales processes that are documented in the ***Sales Analysis Tool Kit*** book have been instrumental in my sales team being able to develop and maintain a systemized approach to marketing to new prospective referral sources. Using these techniques, my team has significantly improved in developing more relationship-based centers of influence."

Scott Durkin – Managing Partner
Howe Insurance Group

"I have worked with Gary Seale and his team for the past ten years. It is great to see this level of insight documented for other owners and managers. The *Sales Analysis Tool Kit* book has my resounding endorsement"

Steve Spaw – Vice President   The EMCOT Corporation – Houston, TX

"Gary Seale is a true sales professional and has incorporated his career's worth of learning in this book. Anyone who is responsible for sales or a sales team can benefit from reading, studying and practicing all that is revealed in his **Sales Analysis Tool Kit**. This book would have been helpful when my team was rapidly growing a legal services company that employed hundreds of sales professionals."

**John Fincher, CBI
Mergers and Acquisitions Advisor**

"In **The Sales Analysis Tool Kit,** Gary Seale peals back the onion and gets to the heart of the sales formula. Most of the time, poor sales results come from a broken concept buried deep within the sales person. **The Sales Analysis Tool Kit** uncovers those broken flaws and empowers your sales machine to make record results! This should be in every Sales Manager's quick reach!"

**Scott Carley – Executive Consultant
The Change Energizer, Austin, TX**

"The Sales Analysis Tool Kit is one of those books that you want to keep within arm's reach at all times. Gary knows that a company's sales team is the engine that drives revenue and success. Building a high performance sales team is Gary's wheelhouse. He's been there and done that. Now, in **The Sales Analysis Tool Kit** book, Gary reveals the secrets, systems, and processes for building a better sales team. "

Dan Forbes, President
Forbes Property Group, LLC., Austin, Texas

TABLE OF CONTENTS

QUESTIONNAIRES

INSTRUCTIONS

Section One

Questionnaires

The following section includes nine different questionnaires and personnel related quizzes. These questions will provide some thought-provoking insight into the sales, marketing and operational side of your business.

Take the time to genuinely scrutinize each segment of your business and determine if your team is performing well or has room for improvement.

The analysis the questionnaires provide should serve as a springboard for improvement and ultimately the financial success of the business.

The SWOT Questionnaire

One of the tools used to analyze the current position of a company and place it in capsule form is called a S.W.O.T. analysis. The acronym stands for Strengths, Weaknesses, Opportunities and Threats. This is a common form used by the senior executives of a company to describe the competitive position of the firm in their quarterly 10k reports. The very same concept can be applied to your sales team.

A description of the category content follows:

- <u>Strengths</u>: A description of the current and future strengths of the team. This could include categories such as experience, product knowledge, market knowledge and close rates. For the company, this could involve product strength in the market, tech advantages, patents, management philosophies, research and development, cash, leverage, market position, pending product releases, customer relationships and international market penetration. All these factors contribute to the success of the sale team or individual.

- **Weaknesses:** Current and future weaknesses might include eroding margins, reduced product demand, technical disadvantages, employee talent depletions, and aging production equipment. For the individual producer, it may mean a failure to keep up with technology, a pessimistic attitude or a loss of focus and energy dedicated to selling the product. It could also simply be a deficiency in selling skills; which can be corrected with training.

- **Opportunities:** Increased market demand, a growing economy, competitor's exit from a market, new product intro, marketing expertise, pending product development, leading technical expertise.

- **Threats:** Patent expiration, new competitors, tax law changes, a weakening economy, loss of a production facility, radical product advantage by a competitor, senior management failures and pending legal actions. For the individual it could be low morale, a change in health or a concern about their future with the company.

The SWOT becomes a form of due diligence for management as they determine the strategies of the company. Performing a SWOT analysis is an excellent example of keeping wisdom in view. It also drives them to focus on opportunities and threats. This focus keeps management from exploring frivolous ventures which are outside the scope of the company and incur unacceptable risks.

With the rapidly changing business environment we operate in today a periodic introspective look at the sales team is absolutely necessary.

The size of the organization should have no impact on the thought process or need to put a SWOT report together. It is an outstanding idea even if you run a small sole proprietorship or a multi-billion dollar organization.

1. What is working well now with the sales production team?

2. Where do you see issues with the current system or performance?

3. How are your sales-oriented software systems working? (CRM System, Sales Results Reporting, Sales History, Trends, Alerts, Inventory Tracking, Order Entry) What brands are installed and working now?

4. Do you have a well written, clearly defined customer target market?

5. On a scale of 1 to 10 how would you rate the quality of your existing sales force? (Verbal skills - persuasiveness, product knowledge, human relations, team player, closing abilities, company and industry knowledge, time management, expense control, confidence, appearance, software skills, other)

6. Do you have a formal new associate onboarding system in place? (Company culture, expectations, product knowledge, industry knowledge, reporting systems, authority levels, etc.) Do you assign mentors?

7. Do you have a realistic perspective of your company's strengths and ability to perform matched with the client base that is targeted?

8. Do you have a personnel evaluation process in place in conjunction with job descriptions and clearly communicated responsibilities?

9. What set of performance metrics exist now for the outside and inside sales team? Minimums established?

10. What type of accountability/reporting program is in place for the sales team?

11. On a scale of 1 to 10 (1 low – 10 excellent) how would you rate the sales leadership as it currently exists?

12. How is the morale in the company? (1= Low to 10 = High) Do they have hope for the future?

13. Are your primary products competitive in your marketplace? (features, benefits, pricing, deliveries, delivery method, support)

14. If applicable, do you offer financing for your product acquisition?

15. Do you have a system for gathering competitive information? How accessible is that information? Explain the system.

16. What is your typical length of time to close an account?

17. Have you established a minimum quote value for sales team to approach?

18. Is there a Pareto Principle / Statistical analysis program in place for your sales results?

19. Are there regular team building meetings and exercises for the company? Frequency?

20. What type of training is available to the sales team? (Mandatory or optional, selling skills, technical skills, business related education) Are they growing in these areas?

21. Do you have a Vision Statement, Mission Statement and clearly communicated set of principles? (Please provide a copy of each statement and the values)

22. What opportunities do you see pending in the future to grow product and service sales? (Acquisitions, marketing push, revised products, new products, additional sales effort, geographic expansion, economic trends, technological innovation, etc.)

23. What threats to your business do you see currently or pending in the foreseeable future? (Technological, competition, product obsolescence, marketing/sales deficiency, production constraints, financial, HR, etc.,)

24. Describe the compensation program in place for your salespeople? Is it fair and equitable to both the employer and salesperson?

25. What is the biggest challenge you are facing in your business?

25B. Why is it important that you find a solution to this challenge now?

25C. What approaches have you tried to solve this issue?

25D. What is it about your challenge that makes it so hard to solve?

26. What are your annual gross sales numbers?

27. What are your gross margin percentages? Do you know the industry average?

28. What is your net profit percentage? Do you know the industry average?

29. How many full-time salespeople are working for the company? If none, please explain.

30. What industry/market do you compete in?

Concerned about where these questions may lead you? Contact Gary Seale at trucon@sbcglobal.net

SMBE Sales Concerns

Small to Medium Business Enterprise   Score
Sheet

Scale: 1 to 5. Total Maximum Points 100

Weak	Fair	Good	Very Good	Excellent
1	2	3	4	5

1. A clearly defined target market	Self-Score Here._____
2. Attitude- Positive, confident- Smile!	Self-Score Here._____
3. A clear differentiation message	Self-Score Here._____
4. Product offering is focused	Self-Score Here._____
5. Sales team is assertive, not aggressive	Self-Score Here._____
6. Owner tasked with all sales and admin duties	Self-Score Here._____
7. Vision statement available to guide the company	Self-Score Here._____
8. Mission statement used to guide daily activities	Self-Score Here._____
9. A digital sales and marketing approach is active	Self-Score Here._____
10. Sales team follows up as they should	Self-Score Here._____
11. Product knowledge, presentation and closing skills	Self-Score Here._____

12. Website content, structure and SEO is viable	Self-Score Here.____
13. Product quality	Self-Score Here.____
14. Sales team interacting with true decision maker?	Self-Score Here.____
15. A coordinated sales and marketing plan	Self-Score Here.____
16. Accountability plan in place	Self-Score Here.____
17. Sales team driven by metrics that does not generate business	Self-Score Here.____
18. Comp plan penalized instead of rewards sales contributors	Self-Score Here.____
19. Sales training and motivation in place for sales team members	Self-Score Here.____
20. CRM in place to track clients, prospects and sales ops	Self-Score Here.____

Total _____

Target Market Identification Questionnaire

Target Market Identification Questions and Statements for B to B Suppliers

Describe your company?

What do you make?

How long have you been in business?

What are your existing product strengths?

What weaknesses should you be concerned about?

Who are your existing customers?

How would you describe these customers? (Size, industry, location)

What geographic areas are you targeting?

1. Pursue similar companies that mimic your existing accounts. Review old account records and pursue those same companies again.

2. Google for the products that your target market produces. Capture those names!

3. Use LinkedIn to obtain names that hold the job titles of the prospects in your target geography. Capture the company name and individual's name. Ask for connections and obtain their contact records.

4. Use Chamber of Commerce guides to identify manufacturers in your area by category.

5. Buy an industrial guide directory to locate prospects.

6. Use a web-based list seller like Sales Genie or Hoovers/D&B to locate and segregate your prospects.

7. Ask for referrals, drive your market area looking for new building construction, read your local business journal for new business announcements, and examine the local chamber of commerce website for new business announcements.

8. What issues do your targeted prospects have?

9. What are these prospects hoping to achieve?

10. Do your products address those issues? Make sure you drive home your differentiating factors.

11. Can you name a title or titles at your target market accounts to ask for?

12. Who has the authority to buy your products at these prospect companies?

13. Size of the prospect?
    A. By number of employees
    B. By gross sales
    C. By industry

14. What is the budget year for these prospects?

15. What macro-economic trends are impacting these prospects?

16. What technological trends are impacting these prospects?

17. Are there seasonal trends you need to be aware of?

18. Are your prospects independently owned?

19. Are your prospects a branch or remote location of a corporate entity? * Often times they will lack authority to make the changes in buying that you need to accomplish.

20. Are you aware of any expansion or contraction plans?

21. Any recent changes in ownership or senior management?

22. How long has the decision maker been in that position?

23. Are there long-term supply contracts in force in your product category?

24. Do you need to register your business with purchasing in order to quote?

25. What capital budget criteria does your prospect have? If you sell large ticket items, make sure you approach prospects a full year in advance of their budgeting period.

26. Does the prospect have internal staff that handles your product category?

27. Does the prospect already produce your product category internally?

28. Inquire about previous use of your product category.

29. Are they interacting with your marketing efforts? (opening newsletters, looking at your website, clicking through on product offers, attending webinars?)

30. Are you aware of the net profit margins for your targeted industry? (Low margins make for very stringent budget constraints)

31. Is your prospect being sold or the subject of a merger?

32. What is the credit rating of your prospect? What kind of payment record do they have?

33. What criteria have they established that your product or company must meet to qualify as a supplier? ANSI Standards, ISO9001, Insurance coverage, UL, etc., etc.

34. Keep in mind that in a larger account, the effort level necessary and barriers will be greater. And the time to break into that prospect will normally be longer than a smaller prospect.

35. Put your target market identification in writing and share it with all of your associates, **especially your sales team!**

** If your prospects fall into an individual consumer category, then do your research by standard marketing demographics.

- Age
- Gender
- Marital status
- Ethnicity
- Income
- Employment status
- Nationality
- Political preference
- Psychographics

Salesperson Interview Questions

1. Product knowledge: Ask specific insider industry questions.

2. Company knowledge: How much do you know about _____?

3. Desire to learn: General education? Major? GPA? Additional courses completed? Independent studies? Interested in new concepts?

4. Corporate adaptability: Previous adherence to corporate standards and culture?

5. Energy level: Applicant response on a scale of 1-100? Commitment to work, i.e. evidence of? What are your natural gifts? (Look for problem solving, people orientation, verbal skills) Any hobbies? (Look for energy level required)

6. Persuasiveness: Observe applicant. How well do they sell themselves? Choice of words and delivery. Note body language.

7. Industry experience: Direct question. Amount of time and successes? Inquire about specific

experience as it relates to the open position. Is their experience on the same level as the open position? Far below? Substantially above?

8. Focus: What methods do you use to focus your efforts?

9. Personal empathy: Tell me how you put yourself in a prospect's shoes?

10. Persistence: Tell me about a time you kept coming back until you won?

11. Financial comprehension: Ask specific questions relating to your industry?

12. Attention to detail: Scrutinize their resume and application. Ask about a time they won because of their attention to detail.

13. Listening skills – Observe word comprehension, facial expressions, body language, delivery recognition, their verbal responses

14. Organization-Personal structure skills: Tell me what tools you use to control your sales efforts?

15. Human relations – judgment skills: When is it important to confront someone? (Look for a

response related to truth versus falsehood, reality versus a lack of reality) When do you turn the other cheek? (Look for an answer that says they can overlook a personal insult or lack of respect)

16. Educational background: Does your company have a criterion? Do they meet the criteria? Are you willing to overlook the criteria based on experience and personal selling skills?

17. Problem solving abilities: Tell me about a time when your problem-solving skills saved an order? How does having a problem challenge you?

18. Relate to a broad spectrum of people: Observe applicant; Ask how they relate to a broad spectrum of socio-economic classes?

19. _Psychological toughness-pragmatic, optimistic, realist: How long does it take you to bounce back from a defeat or significant life changing event? (Look for reality in this answer, small issues-quick bounce back, big issues – need time for recovery)

20. Honesty: When is telling the truth relative to the situation? Look for an unqualified never answer; only exception is life and death-evil versus good exception)

21. Value driven work efforts: How do you decide what to do first, second, third, etc.? (Look for an answer related to closing business, and avoiding urgent but not important demands on their time)

22. Trustworthy: How does truth and timeliness relate to being trustworthy?

23. Conscientiousness: How do you build trust? (Look for an answer that says they have empathy and can anticipate other's needs; then take action steps to fulfill those needs.) Do they do these things on a consistent basis?

24. Timeliness: What is your personal policy regarding time deadlines? Do you always meet your policy guidelines?

25. Quality-thoroughness: How would you describe your personal level of quality? i.e. Your thoroughness on projects, follow-up and paperwork?

26. Sees the big picture: How they, the company and the product offering fit in the overall industry? (This may be an observation based on the other responses)

27. Excellent planner: How does your planning ability help you achieve success?

28. Closer: What methods or questions do you use to move the prospect towards a close? What works best for you?

29. Assertive – not personally aggressive: See question 17 also. Ask what criteria determines if a problem is a personnel issue or a product issue. (Look for answers they say they can address concerns impersonally by looking for answers or options about the product and process, not attacking the person they are working with.)

30. Do they "fit" your organization: (Look for compatibility within the company culture. Ability to get along with other people in a productive manner.)

31. Health – appearance: Physical required by your firm? How did they come dressed for the interview? Personal grooming?
32. Verbal skills – Presentation – Conversation: Direct observation. (Look for the ability to

respond to your questions with concise, direct answers, eye contact, personal connection, no personal hype, or flippancy. Look for proper word usage and breath of vocabulary.)

33. Drive, Desire and Dedication: Look for these three essential elements in the overall responses to your questions.

34. Remember: You cannot ask questions about age, race, or religious preference.

35. Ask for a written essay (minimum 250 words) stating why they are the best candidate for the job.

Through direct questioning, testing and observation determine these attributes:

1. Determine their <u>integrity level</u> – Tell the truth and keep their word

2. <u>Intelligence</u> – Have a strong dose of intellectual curiosity

3. <u>Maturity</u> – Can they handle the heat of battle, handle stress and setbacks, enjoy success with equal parts of joy and humility. Respect the emotions of others. They feel confident but

are not arrogant. Have a sense of humor, especially about themselves.

4. Positive energy – To thrive on action and relish change. Extroverted and optimistic. They make conversation and friends easily. They have enthusiasm, and they love to work and love to play.

5. Ability to energize others. Ability to get people revved up. Having a deep knowledge of the business and strong persuasion skills. Focus and ability to build teamwork and unity.

6. Do they have the courage to make tough yes or no decisions? Watch for indecisiveness, lack of decisions and delays can cause failure.

7. Execution – The ability to get the job done. It means a person knows how to put decisions into action and push them forward to completion, through resistance, chaos, or unexpected obstacles. They know winning is about results.

8. Passion – Heartfelt, deep and authentic excitement about work. Care about other people. They love to learn and row, get a huge

kick when others around them do the same. Passionate about all things in their life.

9. <u>Authenticity</u> – Know who they are. They are likeable people. They communicate well and reach people on an emotional level.

10. <u>To have vision</u> and predict the future. The ability to anticipate the radically unexpected. Having a sixth sense for market changes. Knows about existing competition and new entrants.

11. <u>Surround themselves with people better and smarter than they are.</u>

12. How <u>much resilience to they have</u>? Learn from mistakes, regroup, and then get going again with renewed speed, conviction and confidence. How do they respond when they totally get the wind knocked out of them?

➤ <u>Suggestion</u>: The second interview should be a luncheon away from the office. Place the candidate in a more relaxed environment. Avoid noisy atmospheres, have a sedate, quiet restaurant in mind for this meal. Bring along a trusted associate that has a solid track record of hiring qualified producers. Probe for more details about their qualifications. Observe the way they handle the wait staff. Determine the time frame for separation from their current employer and when they can begin working for you. Ask for questions from the applicant. (Look for self-centered questions versus how can I serve you best questions)

➤ Compensation/benefit questions and answers are best reserved for after the job offer. However, both parties should have a general idea of each other's package requirements before proceeding with the interview process.

• For an interviewing consultation contact Gary D. Seale at 512-219-6677

Salesperson Evaluation Template

Scale 1 to 10

1.	Failing
2.	Weak
3.	Struggling
4.	Below Average
5.	Average
6.	Average/Striving to Improve
7.	Above Average
8.	Good
9.	Superior
10.	Excellent

1. Persuasiveness	Ability to use language to lead the prospect to the next level of agreement	Score____
2. Leadership	Learning to lead themselves & others in a positive direction	Score____
3. Use of CRM Software	Uses CRM tool to max advantage- Creates historical track record and schedules follow ups	Score____
4. Energy-Passion	Deep commitment to learn, exceed goals and communicate	Score____

5. Focus	Ability to stay focused on sales & marketing effort necessary to win	Score___
6. Wisdom	Makes superior long term decisions – Does not set poor precedents	Score___
7. Problem Solving	Dedicates time and energy to diplomatically work issues out for a positive solution	Score___
8. Supplier Relationships	Understands the importance of professional and cordial supportive relationships	Score___
9. Creativity	Uses creative sales techniques, problem solving and individual marketing tools	Score___
10. Competitiveness	Assertive, not aggressive, Acts boldly in closing opportunities	Score___
11. Corporate Adaptivity	Willingness to adapt to the company culture	Score___

12. Personal Confidence	Healthy sense of self -esteem. Aware of their capabilities.	Score___
13. Attitude	The aspect of being positive or negative about their circumstance and the future. Impact on others?	Score___
14. Buy-in	Extent that they support the vision and mission of the company. Believe in the company products and promote them vigorously.	Score___
15. Integrity	Tells the truth, honors their commitments and practices strong ethics.	Score___
16. Sales Adaptability	Ability to relate to a broad spectrum of people and learn new products quickly and thoroughly.	Score___
17. Accuracy	Quality of their reports and assessment of sales potential	Score___
18. Organization	Sales records, Technical information, literature, forms	Score___

19. Planning	Logical? Achievable? Focuses time and energy on best potential	Score___
20. Product Knowledge	Depth of knowledge, How product functions in customer's business	Score___
21. Self-Development	Extends effort to obtain extra education, Grow job skills	Score___
22. Company Knowledge	Understands and utilizes company strengths to grow their business	Score___
23. Industry Knowledge	Understands the industry category and uses information to maintain perspective	Score___
24. Competitive Knowledge	Knowledge & awareness of competitive products and competitors	Score___
25. Account Knowledge	Knows their clients: Products, processes, demands, culture, constraints, authority to purchase, volume potential	Score___

26. Account Penetration	Ability to open new accounts – Opens large accounts with significant potential	Score___
27. Account Industry Knowledge	Knows the industry category of major accounts – Typical constraints, macro and micro issues	Score___
28. Relationship with Peers	Cordial? Professional? Productive? Friendly?	Score___
29. Relationship with Superiors	Respect: Adheres to company guidelines without correction. Humble and cordial	Score___
30. Relationship with Subordinates	No arrogance or disrespect. Fair and professional	Score___
31. Customer Relationship Skills	Pleasing, but firm. Establishes strong connections. Respectful. Seen as a resource. Trusted.	Score___
32. Supervision Required	Minimal amount? Moderate?, Maximum? Earns trust, respect, autonomy.	Score___

33. Probing Skills	Ability to preplan questions and use them in a sales situation to uncover needs	Score___
34. Presentation Skills	Ability to explain, persuade with emotion, handle objections and close at the appropriate time.	Score___
35. Listening Skills	Listens on purpose, senses buying opportunities, does not interrupt	Score___
36. Closing Skills	Knows when and how to close – Close rate generates a viable income	Score___
37. Handles Objections Well	Uses full capabilities to diplomatically answer and overcome objections	Score___
38. Negotiation Skills	Understands when and how. Comes to a successful conclusion	Score___
39. Time and Territory Management	Uses time to focus on income production – Manages travel and schedule to maximize productivity	Score___
40. Follow Up	Timely and assertive. With both internal	Score___

	associates and prospects	
41. Thorough Preparation	Able & willing to be mentally and physically prepared for presentations and prospect engagement and marketing	Score___
42. Coachable	Willing to learn, accept advice and use it in selling activities	Score___
43. Attention to Detail	Alert to sales opportunities, buying cues, acute awareness of product details	Score___
44. Prospecting and Marketing skills	Knowledge & use of prospecting / marketing tools in the marketplace	Score___
45. Close Probabilities	Knows if prospect has need, ability and authority to purchase. Accurate prediction of closed business.	Score___
46. Expense Control	Prudent, Operates within the company guidelines	Score___
47. Goal Achievement	Quotas, profitability, Management By	Score___

	Objectives, product support in the field, account management	
48. Team Player	Willing to assist with company objectives, other salespeople, promotes company agendas	Score___
49. Overall Quality Approach	Commitment to excellence in every aspect of their job responsibilities	Score___
50. Appearance	Clothing, hair, weight, personal hygiene	Score___
51. **Total Score**		

Evaluation Results

450	500	**Excellent**
400	449	**Very Good**
350	399	**Above Average**
300	349	**Average**
200	249	**Weak**
0	199	**Very Weak**

Personality Tests

Ensure that you and your sales team take these tests, review the details with intensity and work diligently to focus on your area of strengths.

*There will be some costs associated with the DISC test results and the books that are recommended.

Tony Robbins DISC

https://www.tonyrobbins.com/disc/

Strengths Finder: Purchase this book and take the cloud-based test to receive your <u>Top Five Personality Strengths</u>. There is a full explanation included about how to use your strengths. Capitalize on your individual strengths and develop them to achieve your maximum capabilities.

Standout also has a cloud-based test that delivers two top personality strengths.

Now, Discover Your Strengths provides an in-depth explanation on how to develop your unique talents and strengths.

The Customer Service Questionnaire

Scale: 1 to 10

1 = Low or poor experience

10 = Superior or excellent experience

1.	Initial Impression	Phone answering, Voice mail system, Receptionist, Office appearance, Phone-Multiple transfers	Score___
2.	Customer Service Reps	Pleasant, Prompt, Well-Informed, Accurate, Experienced, With authority to act	Score___
3.	Website	More than a PR platform, FAQ's, Links to deep instruction. Reference for customers, CSPs, Sales and Mgt.	Score___
4.	Delivery Time	Deliveries clearly communicated, meet or exceed stated dates, Tracking available and communication on delays	Score___
5.	Communication	Genuine two-way communication in every aspect of the sales, delivery and service engagement.	Score___
6.	Restocking and Returns	A policy is in place. CSR's have authority to implement, Applicable charges are communicated	Score___

7. Installation	Technicians are well schooled, courteous, timely and obey all host regulations.	Score____
8. Assembly	Hardware is properly assembled before delivery or onsite to meet or exceed the specifications	Score____
9. Warranty	Is clearly communicated and available. Warranty covers potential issues. Company has the flexibility to extend.	Score____
10. Pricing	Your pricing is competitive, and levels are fairly applied across purchase volumes and the other associated costs involved	Score____
11. Tech Support	The appropriate people, hardware, software and communication systems are in place to maintain your products and address issues.	Score____
12. Education	Systems and people are in place to facilitate pre and post install training	Score____
13. Spare Parts	A reasonable level of spare parts is available to prevent shutdowns and inconveniences for your customers. Legacy products are supported.	Score____
14. Service	Techs are well educated, prepared with the proper tools, Arrive on time, Finish within specified timeframe. Service is available when the customer requires them.	Score____

15. The Transaction Process	How many methods of payment are available? Does your company finance capital purchases? Do you offer prompt payment discounts? What are your terms?	Score____
16. New Account Approval	Credit check process? Length of time to establish an account. Information exchange necessary?	Score____
17. Emergency Service	Quality and availability of software, personnel, replacement parts to meet the customer's demands on a timely basis	Score____
18. CSR Software	A responsive, order system, open orders, transit information, backorders, and pricing is provided. Product information, account status is provided. Work in progress reports.	Score____
19. Outside Representation Experience	Salespeople are knowledgeable and professional. Understands business etiquette, neither pushy nor aggressive. Provide timely quote and follow up responses. They know their products, company and industry.	Score____
20. Ethics	Consistency and integrity are part of the core principles of the company. Commitments are made on purpose and kept. A written set of	Score____

	principles are applicable to all associates.	

Total _____

- A sum total of 100 points is possible. Applaud yourself for strong scores. Look to address issues that may be costing you business.

Sales Leadership Score Sheet

Scale

1. Lacking
2. Sufficient
3. Good
4. Very Good
5. Excellent

Please score yourself as a sales leader in each category and total the points, divide your raw score by 30 to arrive at an average leadership score.

1. Truthful	Score
2. Consistent	Score
3. Experienced	Score
4. Personal Character	Score
5. Competent	Score
6. Confident - Courage	Score
7. Compassionate	Score

8. Persuasiveness	Score
9. Optimistic	Score
10. Humble	Score
11. Sacrificial - Disciplined	Score
12. Trainer - Mentor	Score
13. Organized - Planner	Score
14. Visionary- Plans f/Future	Score
15. Resourceful	Score
16. Decisive – Action Oriented	Score
17. Effective – Establishes Priorities	Score
18. Good Time Manager	Score
19. Recognizes Talent	Score
20. Handles Change Well	Score
21. Practices Confidentiality	Score
22. Recognizes Opportunity	Score
23. Strong Communicator	Score
24. Focused on Business	Score

25. Has a Passion for Business	Score _
26. Positive Attitude	Score
27. Accepts Responsibility	Score
28. Active Learner	Score
29. Stands Up for Their People	Score
30. Knowledgeable – Company, Products and Industry	Score

Total _____

Add your total. Divide by 30 = Average Score

The Morale Test Questionnaire

From a Managerial Perspective

Take this test from a managerial perspective. What can you observe from the conduct of your sales and sales support team?

SCALE

1.	Strongly Disagree
2.	Neither Agree or Disagree
3.	Agree
4.	Totally Agree
5.	Extraordinary – Excellence in Action

Score

1. Put considerable amount of extra time into their work	
2. Rarely take time off, even when it is due	

3. Almost never miss a day of work	
4. Put more effort into work compared to others	
5. Their exhibited energy and intensity are well above average	
6. They show enthusiasm in everything they do. (Great attitude)	
7. They intensely dislike being interrupted during work	
8. Their focus on the sales effort is superior	
9. They lose track of time while they are working	

10. They refuse to be distracted while they are working	
11. They genuinely enjoy their work	
12. They are pleased with their current position	
13. They are not shopping for another position internally or externally	
14. Their overall performance is high	
15. Their sales production is exceeding plan	
16. They volunteer to go the extra mile for the customers and the good will of the company	

17. Their extra effort separates them from the pack	
18. They know what it takes to be excellent and execute that knowledge with excellence	
19. They set very high standards for themselves and strive to adhere to those standards	
20. They choose to work harder and smarter than the average salesperson	

Total Score_____

Competitive Information Research

Word to the wise. Don't spend a lot of time worrying about your competition. Take care of your business first.

Research Questions

1. Conduct a website review. Look at their product offering, staff, inside sales structure, content details, geographic coverage, product lines.

2. Do a Google search for product key words? Who provides what you do? How do they rank organically?

3. Check to see if they are hiring. What positions? Does the frequency of ads indicate turnover or growth?

4. Check for executive team changes.

5. Check pricing for a policy constraint. Do they have published prices available online?

6. How is their sales team structured and assigned?

7. Where are their office locations?

8. Where do they hold and ship inventory?

9. Check out their marketing messages. Tag lines, claims, extra pushes. What culture do they indicate?

10. Search the company on LinkedIn. What is the quality of the profile? How many employees are on LinkedIn? Check the website and electronic catalog for product lines and history.

11. If they are a public company, read their mandatory quarterly reports. (Typically listed under the financial reports on the website)

12. Ask existing clients about these competitors. (Never slam or degrade, stay neutral when you hear the response)

13. Buy company profiles via a professional list company. Example: Hoovers-D&B, Sales Genie.

14. Who are they calling on? Where are they networking?

15. Are they active in Trade Shows as exhibitors?

16. Read press releases if applicable.

17. Do they have customer lists published on their website? Take a look!

18. Public complaints posted in review sites? Yelp, etc.

19. Expansion plans announced?

20. Layoffs happening?

21. Compensation reputation?

22. Marketing notes: Messaging? Content Quality? Frequency?

23. Head count compared to gross sales dollars. (Depending on the industry and profit margins, divide number of employees into gross sales dollars, or multiply employees by $500,000 to approximate gross sales)

24. Customer satisfaction on a scale of 1 to 5?

25. Percentage of market share held?

26. Brand perception in the market?

27. Total market for products? Growth, Flat, Declining?

28. Channel partners in use?

29. Participating in alliances? Purchasing cooperatives?

30. Significant contract gain or loss recently?

31. Participation in trade associations?

32. Gross sales dollars?

33. What are the average margins for the industry?

34. Commodity supplier? Capital goods supplier? Complexity of products represented/manufactured?

35. For a thorough set of formulas as it relates to a sales team and specific to your industry, contact Trucon Consulting for more in depth metrics.

Section Two
Sales and Marketing Instructions

Section two of the book includes instructions on the necessity of having a profit, business to business selling skills and a sales negotiation module.

You will also find a section on ethics, solution selling and the mandatory numbers game. There is information about understanding how to use the DISC personality profile in a sales situation and a LinkedIn mining process.

This information can be used as an introduction to sales for a newcomer or as a refresher for a seasoned professional. Trucon Sales Consulting is available for webinar led sessions or training sessions delivered in person.

Business Basics – Profit Necessity

For those of us that work in today's corporate business world, we all live in the area of specialization. Salespeople are focused on moving product, accountants keep track of revenues, costs and assets, finance personnel work on cash flow and credit issues, production engineering keeps the products coming off the lines, and the personnel department manages people resources and benefits. The list goes on and on. For every individual assigned a role in the company, each one requires a specialized skill that is applauded and fostered by management.

Both the senior management and the small businessperson must focus on:

1. Cash flows

2. Gross margin and net profit

3. Inventory turns

4. Customers and

5. Growth.

Departmental heads and their staff may have more training and expertise in their specialized areas, but they are still not responsible for the overall success of the business. Let's look at each of the five categories and determine why they are so critical.

Cash flow is both a short term and long-term issue that can immediately halt business operations if cash is not available. Sales of the company's products create a receivable account that must be collected within a reasonable amount of time. (usually 30-45 days) The slow collection of receivables can hamper the purchase of additional stock, component parts, personnel salaries and credit repayment. No collection eliminates the essential element of cash flow and profit and stifles all aspects of business operations due to the lack of ability to fund operations. Of course, some amount of retained earnings or lines of credit can alleviate temporary cash flow shortages. But over a long-term basis, viable sales of the company's product lines must be ongoing. To compute the days in receivables, divide gross receivables by net sales divided by 365.

Cash flow is the day to day lifeblood of the firm. Any erosion of the days in accounts payable (time from invoice generation to collection-in days) must be promptly addressed. Poor cash flow issues can be generated in a number of functional areas of a business. The untimely assembly of finished goods, shipping procedures, banking logistics, issuing liberal payment terms and inaccurate invoicing are just a few areas to examine. This critical element must be taken into consideration in every decision made, large or small.

The gross margin and the net profit are the next two essential elements that must be managed. The gross margin is simply the difference between the cost of goods sold and the selling price. The net profit is the cost of goods sold, the cost of operations and taxes subtracted from the gross revenue from the sale of goods, plus other income. Other income might be derived from interest income or the sale of a depreciated asset.

Managing the sales price of goods sold is always a challenge. Marking up product to cover the cost of goods, fixed and variable costs, then include room for net profit is always constrained by competition, market demand and the company's buying power or production efficiencies. These statements regarding the management of fixed expenses, variable expenses and production efficiencies cover substantial amounts of education, experience and discipline required to achieve success in profit management issues. An example in the usage of one dollar of revenue should be instructional here.

Sales Revenue	$1.00
Cost of Goods Sold	< .75>
Operating Costs – Other Expenses	<.17>
Net Income Before Tax	.08
Taxes	<.035>
Net Income	.045

Inventory turns are the third critical component of business basics. Perhaps the best way to understand this concept is to go back to our income statement. The largest percentage of company revenue is dedicated to the costs of goods sold. To manufacture or buy an entire years' worth of product is impractical and foolhardy. Since our theoretical company only nets 4.5 cents per every dollar of revenue, and our goal is to maximize net income, more sales revenue appears to be the easy answer. Therefore, the goal is to sell the existing inventory, collect our accounts receivable and use that 75 cents of revenue to make or buy more viable product. Sounds simple, doesn't it? If only it were easy as these simple steps.

The decisions required here are critical ones. What products to introduce, modify or eliminate? How much inventory should be held? What markets to enter or exit? What customers to approach and how to approach them? What investments to make in plant and production equipment? Or, do you outsource the manufacturing?

In light of all these decisions, inventory turns must be achieved to drive the profitability of the company. Although the percentage of net profit will stay the same, the volume of dollars earned will increase as turns go up. As an additional input into your business basics lesson, it can easily be seen that minimizing expenses can have a real impact on bottom dollar profitability. That is why you will experience a constant drive to maximize efficiency and limit spending in the business world.

Companies with high percentage net profits can be a little less stringent with turns requirements and still survive. However, narrow margin industries such as retail grocery and electronic contract manufacturing must be very concerned about turns. With 1-2% net margins, seemingly minor errors can quickly lead to red ink baths. (To compute inventory turns, divide the cost of goods sold by the average inventory held)

An understanding of this concept allows us to quickly understand why slow moving or "dead stock" inventory becomes such a high priority to senior management. Our 75 cents that we were relying on to pay for new sellable products is tied up in inventory setting on the warehouse shelf. Or in the case of perishable inventory, rotting in the storeroom.

Customer relations are the fourth critical area of business concerns. Understanding the macro and micro needs of your client base is essential knowledge for almost every aspect of the seller's business. The product mix, pricing, delivery, payables and international compatibility are just a few areas that must be understood.

Feedback from the sales staff, the marketing department, and other functional areas of the company that have client contact can be valuable sources of information. Research, reading industry publications, business publications and involvement of the senior management are critical components of staying close to the customer as well.

The fifth essential element is growth. Even though a few small businesses have a stated goal of no growth, it is rare. In the corporate world, it is unheard of. Growth fuels the requirement to cover additional profits, secure investors, attract quality people, secure financing and enhance morale. Growth also involves a strong need for competitive products at a competitive price. In a number of instances, growth means the survival of the company due to the need for the economies of scale to be competitive.

As you can see, the five categories are interconnected because they are co-dependent. Without customers, we have no business. Without profit and cash flow, we collapse as a company. Unless we turn our inventory, cash is frozen and profit volume is intolerably low. Without growth, stagnation sets in that isolates us from the vital aspects of the business community and we die internally as well as externally.

Application: As an employee, manager or proprietor, have you lost focus on these five essential elements? If the answer is yes, put things in perspective. Look at the big picture and refocus your actions while there is still time.

Business To Business Sales Foundations

The Guide to a Foundation of Success
In Your Selling Career

Trucon Sales Consulting

Austin, Texas
www.truconbd.com
512-219-6677

Table of Contents

- Meyers Briggs Test
- Product Knowledge
- Employer Capabilities
- Feature Advantage Benefit
- Market Identification
- Probing
- Top Level Contact
- Presentation
- Handling Objections
- Sales Negotiation
- Closing
- Time and Territory Management
- Reporting
- Ethics
- Summary

Introduction to Sales

Goal

The goal of this course is to provide the student with a comprehensive outline of the skills and methods necessary to achieve success in the competitive field of personal selling. This fundamental program allows the individual new to the field of selling to grasp the preparation level necessary to be competitive and nullify the myths surrounding a sales career. This material is a tried and proven formula for account penetration and retention.

1. Steps in the Selling Process

1. Prospecting

2. Preparation – Planning the Sales Call

3. Probing and Presentation

4. Overcoming Objections

5. Obtaining Commitment

6. Building a Long-Term Relationship

Prospecting: Is the process of <u>locating potential customers</u>. This is a critical activity because customers switch suppliers, move out of the market area, go out of business, are acquired or have a one-time need for the product. There are two major activities:

1.) Locate the prospects
2.) Screen the prospects for need, authority to purchase, ability to pay, volume, demand on your time, etc.

Planning the Call: Salespeople should have:

1.) Thorough company knowledge
2.) Technical and commercial product knowledge
3.) Competitive product knowledge
4.) Market knowledge
5.) Knowledge of the prospect

Probing and Presenting: Use open and closed probes. Present to the concerns of the customer. Be well prepared with literature, technical information, be adaptable, have a call purpose, reinforce key points, be detail minded, be open to questions, make the presentation a performance, be open to questions, keep your perspective and enjoy the presentation, sell, not converse.

Overcoming Objections: Expect objections. Expect objections at any time. Objections to appointments, during presentation, during the closing process and even after sale follow up. Common Objections: No need, need more information, new concept, not interested, doesn't understand, doesn't like product, company or salesman, no money, cost exceeds value, expects price concession, deals primarily with a competitor, wants more time to consider the offer.

Obtaining Commitment: The salesperson must <u>ask for a commitment</u>. Be persistent, ask several times. Review the benefits and drawbacks to not having the product. Ask for the order and wait for a response. Assure the customer they have made <u>the right decision</u>. Show sincere appreciation for the order. Analyze the no's for cause.

Build a Long-Term Relationship: Very important. <u>Establish</u> and maintain a customer <u>information file</u>. Monitor order placement. Ensure the <u>proper use of the product</u>, provide ongoing guidance and suggestions on the use of the product. Analyze and <u>respond quickly </u>to questions or complaints. Conduct satisfaction research and respond to the feedback.

2. Qualifications of a Salesperson

No one individual personality type, style, or educational background is ideally suited for a selling occupation. Contrary to popular opinion, the individual salesperson does not need to be an absolute extrovert. As a matter of fact, some people who may not be remotely close to being an extrovert can succeed in sales. However, they may approach their work in an unconventional manner and use a higher level of energy to find success.

As a rule a successful salesperson will have a high level of energy, enjoy people, be reasonably well organized, practice thorough, consistent follow-up, practice honesty, is verbally persuasive and is willing learn the product as well as their market.

1. Do a Meyers-Briggs Test

* Go to. **http://hunanmetrics.com**

This website allows you to take the Meyers-Briggs (Jung) test free of charge and receive a review of potential career choices.

3. Product Knowledge

Product knowledge is one of the essential elements of preparation required for every salesperson. As a representative of your company, the customer may see you alone as the company, regardless of how large or small your supporting organization is. Therefore, your knowledge is critically important to the company's prospects of obtaining the order and your professional image.

Product knowledge is expressed in terms of features. A feature is a distinct or outstanding part of the quality of the product.

Features can be learned by:

1. Having others present the product to you
2. Sales literature
3. Hands on usage or observing usage
4. Instruction manuals
5. Schools, seminars
6. Books
7. C.D.s
8. Datalinks, Internet

9. Having a mentor
10. Teaching others the information

Why is product information important?

1. To sell the product
2. Communicate with the prospect
3. Win over the competition
4. Earn respect, trust, repeat appointments
5. Earn repeat business
6. Promote professional image
7. Avoid repeat calls
8. Avoid embarrassment
9. Understand how the product functions

Exercise: List five features of your primary product.

1.
2.
3.
4.
5.

List five features you bring to your customers:

1.
2.
3.
4.
5.

Obtain a piece of product literature or instruction manual for one of your products and list five key features.

1.
2.
3.
4.
5.

Summary

Product knowledge is an essential foundation that a salesperson must obtain. Simply learning the tangible features of your product offering is not enough. It is important to understand how your product provides service and solves problems for the potential client. Understanding how to present these features will be described in a later section of this training module. A salesperson that fails to obtain product knowledge is virtually guaranteeing a career of mediocrity.

4. Employer Capabilities

Definition: Capability is the ability to accomplish a task. Your employer's capabilities are an important aspect of your ability to close a sale. The prospect may place the support functions that the selling organization provides very high on the list of criteria necessary to earn their business.

Exercise: List five capabilities of your employer as feature statements:

1.
2.
3.
4.
5.

The importance of knowing your employer's capabilities can be as important as knowing the product offering. In some instances, such as service or insurance companies, the product may be so similar to the product offering that a prospect will be unable to differentiate them.

It should be part of your job responsibility to search out and learn the capabilities of your firm that is combined with the product itself to make a total delivery. Determine company abilities that can distinguish you from your competitors. Also look for aspects of your offering that satisfy the emotional needs of your prospect as well as the tangible requirements.

Ask about the following aspects of your company if your employer has not already supplied them:

1. Financial stability
2. Commitment to the marketplace
3. Service levels – time and geographic availability
4. Technical expertise
5. Repair capabilities

6. Parts availability
7. Shipping – delivery capabilities – accuracy
8. Service hours
9. Warranty
10. Depth and breadth of inventory
11. Time to process an order
12. External training for customers
13. Rental products
14. Lease – purchase
15. Financial capability
16. Quality of products carried
17. Experience of staff personnel
18. Computer capabilities
19. Engineering capabilities
20. Information availability – Catalogs, web site, e-mail, papers written, seminars, newsletters

One aspect of selling that you cannot forget is that you become a company capability as soon as you interface with a prospective client. In that situation you "become the company" to your customer. Your knowledge conduct and responsiveness to fulfilling your customer's needs make the salesperson a vital link in providing information services to your prospects. Knowledge is power. You owe it to yourself and your employer to obtain all the power necessary to become a winner in the marketplace.

As a result of downsizing, the drive for profitability, and the assessment capabilities of your clients, the need to differentiate your offering has frequently become the difference between winning and losing business. Therefore, the benefits of your product and your ability to tie the capabilities of your company into the selling process has become a critical skill.

5. Feature, Advantage, Benefit

Stating the <u>feature</u>, the advantage to that <u>feature</u> and a benefit that <u>feature</u> delivers is a superior method of presenting your product. This is called the **FAB** method.

The reasons to use the fab method are:

1. So the prospect will <u>understand</u>
2. So the prospect will <u>agree</u>
3. So the prospect will <u>take action</u>

A **feature** is something you can:

1. <u>See</u>
2. <u>Touch</u>
3. <u>Measure</u>

It is expressed as a noun. Detailing a feature answers the question, "What is it?"

An Advantage is:

The advantage is a performance characteristic of the feature. It answers the question. What will the feature do?

The Benefit is:

A benefit is an asset characteristic expressed as a personalized value. It answers the question. What does the product do for my company or me? People make decisions based on both logical and emotional criteria. Therefore, there are two types of benefit statements.

Logical: Stated in dollar terms or some other quantifiable basis

Emotional: Stated in personal terms

The logical aspect of a benefit:

1. Makes money
2. Saves money
3. Saves time
4. Makes time available
5. Increases productivity
6. Improves quality

The emotional aspect of a benefit:

1. Provides recognition
2. Denotes achievement
3. Provides security
4. Promotes personal profit
5. Reduces worry
6. Provides personal pleasure
7. Reduces the hassle factor

What can you FAB?

1. Product
2. Company
3. Service
4. Program
5. Yourself

To determine which features to focus on, find out what motivates your prospect. Look at the "big picture." In other words, what national or global

influences are taking place? How is your competition positioned? What do you know about the plant or the industry as a whole? What have you learned from other staff members at the customer's facility?
Reasons to develop benefits

1. Answers the number one question: "What's in it for me?"
2. Appeals to the prospect's individual needs, wants, concerns and future plans.
3. Feature and advantages only – imply benefits.
4. Features and advantages only – invite comparison.
5. Benefits are reasons for agreeing.
6. Benefits are reasons for **Buying.**

Exercise: Refer back to the product literature you used to write the five features. Now write five feature, advantage and benefit statements regarding that product.

FAB statements:

1.

2.

3.

4.

5.

Write a personal features list. After you compile your features list, write three FAB statements you might have used when you interviewed with your sales manager.

Potential list profile:

1. Education
2. Honors
3. Previous experience
4. Achievements
5. Communication skills
6. Technical skills
7. Analytical skills
8. Creativity
9. Persistence
10. Maturity

Three personal FAB statements:

1.

2.

3.

Exercise:

Take your product FABs and personal FABs and review them with your sales manager. Ask for constructive feedback on the accuracy of your FABs.

Evaluation Criteria

1. Were the features real features?
2. Were the advantage statements advantages or benefits?
3. Were the benefits believable?
4. Did the FAB statements demonstrate strong product knowledge?
5. If the product was technical, was the salesperson able to present clearly to a less knowledgeable person?
6. Did the salesperson appear confident as they made their benefit statements?

6. Market Identification

Now that we have established a method for knowing your product and product presentations, how do we know what industries and individuals to actively call on?

Exercise: In the space provided below describe how you would identify your primary customers?

Market Identification Aids

1. Existing customer lists
2. Similar businesses
3. Chamber of Commerce guides
4. Professional Associations and membership lists
5. Business Journals
6. LinkedIn Mining
7. Purchased list Ex: D & B, Sales Genie databases
8. Manufacturer leads
9. Cold call prospecting
10. Websites
11. Word of mouth - Networking
12. Ask existing customers
13. Internet Research via Search Engines

Use demographics

A. Income
B. Age
C. Housing area
D. Occupation/Title
E. Education
F. Number of Children/ages
G. Religion
H. Sex

Do some initial research on one of your company's "typical" customers/accounts. Write a profile of this account.

The prospect is the most important individual involved in selling your product. You owe it to yourself and your company to call on the actual decision-makers. One of the serious mistakes that newcomers to the selling field make is to present to the first person who will listen to their presentation. This common error leads us to the topic called probing. The probing section will guide you through the important skills required to obtain the customer's requirements. Once these requirements are known, the selling process can proceed.

Probing

What does the term "probing questions" mean to you?

The goal of questioning is to discover information regarding the most important need.

The benefits you receive from questioning are:

1. Knowledge of the prospective client and the company
2. Attitude – Interest
3. Aptitude – experience
4. Personality – How the prospect answers
5. Up to date information on their current needs
6. Conserves your time
7. Determine local influences
8. Determine big picture influences

Questioning Techniques

1. OPEN – Who, What, Where, When, Why, How

2. REFLECTIVE – You - - You are

3. CONTROLLED – Negative - - Positive

4. CHOICE – Can - - Do You

OPEN Questions

1. Are used to: Obtain a customer's point of view and obtain more information.
2. Cannot be answered with a yes or no.
3. Start with the words: Who, What, Why, When, Where, How

Example:

Ask: When does your budget year end?
Listen: So, you can identify the purchasing deadline.

Then ask: What products do you need budgetary pricing for?
Listen: So, you can narrow the need down to specific products.

REFLECTIVE Questions:

1. Are used to: Emphasize the positive and get rid of the negative.

2. Should not be used unless the customer has agreed with a portion of your proposal.
3. Could be used when the prospect has accepted positive and negative portions of the proposal.

Example:

Prospect: "I can see some values in your Dell lap-top computer, but I don't think I want to go to the extra expense."

Sales Representative: (Positive) "What are some of the things you like about the lap top we are looking at now?"

Sales Representative: "You mentioned the larger hard drive, isn't that important to you."

CONTROLLED Questions:

1. Are used to: Let prospects know you understand their point. To encourage prospects to tell you what they think about the product. To clarify understanding or differences.
2. Can be used if you listen vigilantly.
3. Usually begins with: "You feel" "You are concerned" Use the prospect's own words to feed the question back to them.

Example:

Prospect: "I'm always interested in reducing costs, but I have to be sure my deliveries are on time."
Sales Representative: "You're concerned about on time delivery?"

CHOICE Questions (Closed Probes)

1. Are used to: Check for understanding, obtain <u>information</u>, and guide conservation.
2. Can be answered with a yes or no.
3. Start with the words: "Do you" "Can we" "Which"

Example:

"Do you see how this could fit into your incentive program?"

"Is this your primary area of concern?"

"Can we justify the higher initial cost; is that the question?"

Helpful Hint: Never begin the fact-finding stage of your presentation with choice questions. It is a sure way to eliminate opportunities and paint your way into a corner before your product or service has a chance to be understood.

Finding the Top-Level Contact

Be careful to determine who the true decision_maker for your product is. Do not spend your valuable time and energy presenting to the wrong person in the consumer's organization. It is true that you may have to present to several layers of people or a committee, however it is still important to determine who they may be. Don't forget to ask who makes the final decision and what the bidding policies are for your prospect's company. Be discerning; individuals will tell you they make the decisions when in fact they do not. Typically, a series of open and closed probing questions will help you find out whom you should be talking to.

Examples:

Who writes the specification?
Does this requirement go to the purchasing department for bidding purposes?
Who buys that commodity?
Do you make the final decision on brand and vendor? If not, who does?
Who would make the decision to change products?

Exercise:

Have your sales manager or partner in training assist you in selecting a product from your company's offering to practice with. Have them select four top criteria for buying that product. They should not reveal their criteria. Prepare for a few moments and then go through a probing question interview to determine the four criteria they have chosen.

If you have difficulty finding the four criteria during this exercise, select another product and repeat the exercise until the questioning techniques feel more natural.

8. Presentation

Because of your training and probing skills, you now have a knowledge of your product, your company and your client's needs. Your challenge is to take the client's needs and present your product in the most favorable and attractive light possible while still maintaining your integrity.

Take some time to review the steps in the selling process detailed in section one of this booklet. If the prospect of presenting to a live prospect frightens you, there are several things you can do to calm your nervous feeling.

1. Prepare a list of simple questions to ask the prospect. This replaces a one-sided speech with a conversation. Use open-ended questions first and then narrow down the probes to obtain specific information.

2. Jot down the answers. This makes the client feel important and allows you to refer to your notes without being forced to use total recall.

3. Present primarily to the client's needs. This eliminates the need to go through an expansive list of features; some of which the prospect has no interest in. This focus takes the pressure off of you.

4. Know your product and its applications in great depth. Practice, practice, practice. Repetition builds memory and confidence. Develop a systematic way to present the product. Do not "jump around" as product features come to mind.

5. Seek agreement from the client as you present the items they expressed interest in. Develop a series of Feature, Advantage and Benefit statements to

use for each product feature. This alleviates self-focus and builds to an eventual yes.

6. Be prepared for an **objection**. Prepare to answer objections in advance by covering them in the presentation.

7. Be thoroughly prepared with literature, pricing, technical information and working demo products.

8. If time constraints have not allowed you to prepare properly, present with a power point presentation. Or, use your company's web site to open the presentation with a capabilities overview.

Helpful Hint: Do not read or spew a memorized speech onto your prospect. However, using a memorized opening of 90 seconds will allow you to get over the initial surge of nervousness and the remainder of the presentation can flow smoothly.

You want the prospect's attention to be focused on you since you know what needs to present and in what order it should be addressed. Therefore, do not hand out literature before your presentation or give them a sample of the product to look over while you try to talk.

Finally, relax and enjoy the give and take of the interaction. There is plenty of time to judge your performance after the customer visit.

Setting Appointments

1. Always identify yourself and your company at the start of the phone conservation.

2. Position the call. Example: "I am calling to set an appointment to discuss your .... needs."

3. Request a specific time: Example "If at all possible, I would like to visit with you next Thursday at nine in the morning; if that is a bad time, how does three in the afternoon sound? No? I can appreciate how busy you are. Would Friday or early next week be a better time for you?

4. State, "My goal is to get an opportunity to earn your business." There should be no guessing why you are coming.

5. Since you are calling for a personal appointment, don't sell the product over the phone. Only sell the appointment. Only reveal enough information to interest the prospect, so they will agree to the appointment.

6. After the prospect agrees to a specific time and date, restate that time so that it perfectly clear when you will arrive. "Thank you, I'm looking forward to meeting you in person. I'll see you Thursday morning the 24th at 9 AM."

7. The same approach can be used with e-mail. You will find that for many prospects, e-mail is the

preferred manner of communicating. The same level of courtesy and communication skills can be used to bring the sale to a close.

9. Handling Objections

The process of selling is not merely finding a qualified prospect and reciting a laundry list of features until the prospect buys, but it is a series of responses to the prospect's demands. Almost without exception, the prospect will have an objection. The objection may be stated or not. It will be your job and a measure of your success to determine what those objections are and overcome them so the prospect will be willing to make a purchase decision.

The terms of a purchase are the same terms as a legal contract. There must be something of value (product or service), exchanged for a medium (the price), under some terms and conditions (delivery time, warranty, payment terms, service provided, etc.).

Let's review four aspects of the selling agreement and possible steps to overcome objections to these conditions. These common objections are:

1. Price
2. Wrong feature (color, size, options, etc., etc.)
3. Delivery
4. Service (warranty, training, repairs, parts availability, downtime, etc.)

The Price Objection

1. Go back and obtain another agreement on features, advantages and benefits. Make sure the customer is comparing like products.
2. Break the cost down into the lowest possible element. By year, month, or day.

3. Restructure the payment plan. Down payment, length, interest rate, cash discount.

4. Use third party references

5. Summarize all parts into a close.

Helpful Hint: Overcoming objections is not negotiating. It is part of the selling process. Do not negotiate for less than the maximum agreement possible at this time. Negotiating is necessary only after all the objections have been uncovered and have not been overcome with the benefits of the product alone.

The Wrong Feature or Product Objection

1. Find a similar product with the feature the customer requires.
2. Emphasize the other features the customer likes.
3. Point out cost savings in the product without the feature.
4. Make obtaining the product with the desired feature difficult.
5. Make a small concession or tradeoff to close the sale.

Helpful Hint: Read your prospect carefully. At times the objection is not serious. They may have dropped an inadvertent comment which they would have difficulty remembering. There is a possibility that you should not address the objection or ask to retain it until after the presentation is finished and the concern will be overcome by the other benefits of the product.

The Delivery Objection

1. Place the delivery date in writing; guarantee it.
2. If scarcity is a concern, use the knowledge of scarcity to convince the customer that you will do everything possible to secure a timely delivery.
3. Admit tardiness, offset with FAB statements.
4. Use a different delivery method.
5. Offer a substitute product to meet the delivery deadline.

Overcoming Service Objections

1. Written warranty
2. Reveal more details on your service facility
3. Detail the number of service people, their training, and the average time of response.
4. Use close geographic location to calm concerns.
5. Provide strong brand name products.
6. Use third party references.
7. Provide toll free service calls or secure web site access to techs.
8. Provide loaner or rental equipment in case of down times.
9. Introduce the customer to the technicians.
10. Give the prospective client a tour of your service facility.

Exercise: Have your sales manager or fellow sales associate pick several common objections for a product you will be presenting on a regular basis. Practice discovering the objections and overcoming them with your knowledge of the product and your company support.

10. Sales Negotiations

Definition: An exchange of offers and information between two parties that wish to exchange something of value. It is not a debate. The process will not work if either or both sides are entrenched in their positions.

When to Negotiate

Only when all attempts at utilizing the selling process have failed to reach an agreement.
The sales call should closely resemble this outline.

1. Introduction
2. Probing
3. Presentation
4. Overcome objections
5. Negotiate if necessary
6. Close

Power: If you can give something or take away something the other party desires, you can have power over that person. The other party has to grant you that power.

Example: Buyer/Seller, Parent/Child, Manager/Subordinate

Webster's definition of power: The capacity to exert force, to act with force or vigor. The ability to control others through authority or influence.

Commitment is a key ingredient in sales negotiation.

1. Strongly believe in the worth of your product.
2. Establish targets and goals.
3. Be committed to your goals; be aware of the precedents you may be setting.
4. Prepare options. Be prepared to walk away.

Negotiation Tips:

1. Probe extensively to learn the other parties' real wants and needs.
2. Knowledge is power. Use the knowledge you have to withhold or add to the agreement desired.
3. The selling side should start with the highest quality and price.
4. Buyers should ask for the maximum in price reductions and concessions.
5. Have numerous options prepared. Best, Better, Sufficient, Walk-Away.
6. Every item is negotiable until it is eliminated.
7. Maximize profit or savings
8. Walk-away if is a bad deal for you and your company but preserve the relationship.

Helpful Hint: Watch your choice of words carefully during a negotiation. Refuse to use absolute words concerning the relationship. Do not use weak words, such as hope, wish, maybe, kinda, or phrases such as "I don't know." Be firm, but polite. If you must turn down an offer, do it with regret and a pleasant expression on your face. Do not use strong, negative body language that communicates anger or distrust.

Successful Negotiators:

1. Accommodate to preserve relationships
2. Collaborate to solve problems
3. Compromise to split the difference
4. Withdraw to protect themselves
5. Defeat others when we want to win and cannot compromise

Exercise: Have your sales manager select two items from a list of a product's terms and deliverables that they will not agree to in a sales situation. Discover the two items and negotiate the differences.

11. Closing

Closing is simply the action of bringing the selling process to the next highest level on the decision hierarchy (listed below) or actually obtaining the order from the customer. It is important that the salesperson realize that moving the sale along toward a final close is the objective. It may be very unrealistic to assume that a purchase order can be obtained after one presentation. The decision hierarchy helps us to understand where we are in the closing process.

The Decision Hierarchy

Perspective	Conduct
Acceptance	Entrust
Play	Eager
Proceed	Interested
Consideration	Reserved
Look	Indeterminate
Challenge	Antagonistic
Stop	Opposed
Avoid	Fearful
Complain	Concern
Neglect	Detached

The entire selling process, from initial introduction to final presentation of the product should be focused on bringing the buyer to a purchasing decision. The result of your efforts should be oriented around building trust, obtaining information and presenting your product offering in such a manner that your prospect is constantly agreeing to your FAB statements with a yes answer.

To obtain this continuing span of yes answers, you must ask positive, leading, affirmative questions during the presentation. The answers you get will confirm the feedback you received during the probing process.

For example, after your series of FAB's ask:

Do you agree?
Isn't that what you said you needed?
Wouldn't that improve your productivity/processes?

This product will provide you with the reliability you said was necessary, isn't that correct?

If you are not at a position of final closure, agreement on the next step in the process is necessary. For example, these criteria may need to be met to continue:

1. Time, date, and location of the next meeting.
2. Supply technical data or drawings
3. Product modifications available, or new product offering
4. Who should be in attendance at the next meeting?
5. Pricing details provided
6. Payment terms finalized
7. Delivery/packaging information
8. References supplied
9. Credit information exchanged
10. Level of services required by the customer
11. Volume of product required by the customer
12. Trial period for product to perform as promised or be evaluated

After you know the exchange of information has ended, then there are a number of verbal phrases that can be used to ask for the order. They include:

- Should we obtain a P.O. number now?
- Can you authorize delivery now?
- Where do you want it delivered?
- Have you arrived at a decision?
- When can we start? May I have your signature on this order form?

Closing

Avoid the words buy or sold to the client. People like to make informed purchasing decisions. They do not like to "be sold" by a salesperson.

The final agreement should be in writing if at all possible. It should be in the form of a contract. A contract must:

1. Contain an offer
2. Be accepted
3. Be for some type of consideration
4. Be between competent parties of legal age

Make sure your agreements are:

1. In writing (a legitimate Purchase Order)
2. Identify involved parties
3. Spell out terms and conditions
4. Include signatures of responsible, qualified individuals   Example: Employed by the client firm, proper position to conduct business for the client

Closing exercise: Go back and review the Decision Hierarchy. Convince your sales manager or exercise partner to hire you as their first salesperson. List your agreement terms in the space below.

12. Time and Territory Management

Perhaps no element of the selling profession is so important, yet so overlooked and neglected as the time and territory management aspect of the salesperson's responsibilities. Since the typical outside salesperson has more freedom than an office bound employee, the potential for the abuse of this freedom will always exist. However, this is not the primary concern. The majority of people that earn outside sales positions genuinely want to succeed. Therefore, they are willing to work, and often prefer to work hard without close supervision.

However, the mere task of staying busy can be a trap of mediocrity for the new salesperson. The ability to focus on the highest income producing activities is often a skill that takes years to acquire. But, with a few simple tips and some skill sharpening, a higher level of accomplishment is achievable in this critical area.

A few basic tools are necessary for assistance in this area. Since your position often requires travel, an annual calendar with places for notes and critical phone numbers is important. In the place of business card notebooks, a computer with software programs such as ACT! or Microsoft Outlook in conjunction with Microsoft Office is a significant time saver as well as projecting the image of professionalism you require. These programs not only act as an electronic Rolodex, but also provide the option of creating a call record that becomes invaluable as times goes along. With these tools, you can schedule calls, callbacks, conduct correspondence, create histories and reminders for important due dates that would otherwise have to be done manually. It is also suggested that you have an e-mail account with a major provider that allows you to access your mail in the office and during travel.

Although the creation of a database and its upkeep is often a slow, tedious task, it will pay significant dividends for the entire period you are responsible for the territory.

Time and territory management directives are difficult to generalize due to the vast differences in industries, products promoted, profit margins and the sales cycle time required to close a piece of business. However, many sales jobs can be viewed as a funnel. There must be a substantially larger amount of client contact and presentations given to provide the company with a enough business to support the sales representative and achieve a profit for the company. As your basic economics classes taught you, the goal is to minimize expense and maximize profit. In similar fashion, your goal is to focus on profitable accounts and maximize profit.

This does in fact mean, relegating some client contact and support activity into a secondary position. This is a difficult skill and bears more discussion. This does not mean that you bluntly inform the lower volume or margin client that they are no longer worth your time. Simply placing them on your calendar that allows for some less expensive way of supporting and soliciting their business is preferred. It may be possible to delegate a small account to a telemarketer, mail them materials or direct them to your company web site, thereby eliminating the need for a personal visit.

Since refusing to see a customer with a direct request for assistance runs counterintuitive to most salespeople's basic nature, let's examine the value of your time. To do this we must make several assumptions regarding income and the dollar value of your territory. However, it will be easy to adjust the numbers to fit your specific situation.

Base pay	$50,000
Commission Potential	$25,000
HR Costs	$21,000
Territory Expenses	$16,000
Total	$112,000
Territory Quota	$1,500,000

Assuming five weeks per year are consumed with vacation, holidays, training, travel and trade shows, that leaves 47 weeks per year for direct selling activities.

Assuming that you can make 25 quality contacts per week via phone, fax, e-mail or in person then your time is worth $95 per customer contact.

(47 Weeks x 25 Contacts = 1,175 $112,000/$1,175 = $95)

Your time becomes even more valuable if the total territory quota is used as the dividend.

$1,500,000/1,175 contacts = $1,276 per contact. Granted these are gross numbers, but if we assume 30% gross profit numbers the dollar volume necessary per contact is $383.

These figures and logic should help you place the value of your time in perspective. You simply cannot afford to spend your time with small volume accounts and hope to generate enough revenue to satisfy your income needs and the needs of your employer.

The Pareto Principle states that 80% of your revenue will be generated by 20% of your customers. Although these numbers may be not accurate for every industry, they substantially reflect the way most sales territories look. Therefore, sales records will be a good way to assist in determining where you will spend your time. Past records of individual contacts are a valuable tool also. Spend some time researching the customer base that matches your product with the needs of the prospective customers to assist with the direction of your efforts.

In addition, it is your job to qualify the prospect regarding their willingness to buy, ability to pay and quantity of product they might purchase. These aspects are all part of the territory management responsibility.

The following scenarios should provide a picture of the effort and time required to develop and run a successful territory.

Insurance Sales

In life insurance sales, a good year will result in 80 to 100 whole life policies being sold. Assuming two closes for every five presentations, then 250 presentations need to be given every year. If the close ratio increases, then the number of presentations can decrease. If it takes approximately 14 contacts to achieve one personal appointment, then it would take a minimum of 2,500 attempts to set up 250 appointments.

With this type of raw data, the sales representative can now begin to determine the amount of time and effort required to achieve success.

Divide the amount of time consumed making cold calls, studying, designing and mailing solicitations, setting up and traveling to appointments, making presentations, preparing for follow up, and handling paperwork then you can easily see a full years-worth of 45-55 hour weeks.

Industrial Distributor Sales

This type of sales position will include prospecting, account management activities and carrying out account penetration strategies. Depending upon the level of inside sales support, the outside salesperson can plan to spend 8-16 hours of prep time and follow-up work in the office per week and 24-32 hours in the field engaged in direct selling activities.

It is easy to get caught up in a numbers game with industrial sales. Benchmarks such as 20-25 personal calls per week can be excellent or they can become a downfall. It is much better to ascertain which activity will produce revenue and base your customer contact on the income aspect rather than call numbers. For example, in a $1,500,000 territory there may be 8 accounts that make up 80% of the territory revenue. ($1,200,000) The total territory may be producing

$360,000 in gross profit, and the 8 top accounts produce $288,000 of that amount.

Therefore, if a product usage survey is necessary in one of your large accounts which consumes 18 hours of your workweek yet has the potential to gain an extra $50,000 dollars-worth of business, do it! This is a much superior use of your time than spending those 18 hours with the bottom 80% of your accounts which cannot produce the $50,000 and can easily consume more time than their revenue contribution can support.

It is recommended that you take some time to determine the total income potential per account for the products your company provides. Then find out what percentage of that potential is achievable for you during the upcoming year. *Be realistic*, your competition may have a 2-year contract for a specific commodity or be in a superior cost position for a particular item. Based on these findings, develop an account strategy that will help you reach goals that are fair and reasonable.

As a generalization, many companies divide their account list into A, B, C, and D account categories. "A" accounts are the ones currently producing or have the potential to produce hundreds of thousands of dollars. "B" accounts have less current income or potential (Ex. $100,000 or less). "C" and "D" accounts typically have potential of $10,000 or less per year.

In your analysis, it may be helpful to categorize your accounts to assist in prioritizing your time. As a rule of thumb, " A" accounts may be assigned a call volume of 4 times month, "B" accounts are targeted for 2-3 calls per month and "C-D" accounts are on demand, used to fill in time and managed with direct mail, telemarketers and catalogs.

Cracker Jack Salesperson?

Several years ago, when this author was new to sales, my beginning class of salespeople was shown a short videotape of a new salesman who determined that he could make it big in sales by cramming more into his day. His reasoning was; more presentations, more orders. The tape showed him rushing through preparation work, questioning exercises, pushing for orders and rushing on to the next call. The next scene showed a crowd at a football stadium and above the crowd could be heard shouts of Cracker Jacks! Cracker Jacks! When the camera focused on the vendor, (you guessed it) it was our new salesman who had worked himself to the bottom of the profession. So, the little lesson here is, take time management seriously. Do not become so frenzied that you destroy yourself, family life and your career by assuming that more is always better.

As you begin to schedule yourself for a workday, think logically about the amount of time necessary to drive to the account, contact your client, make the presentation and arrive at the next call on time. Plan to be 10 minutes early to find the lobby and have your contact called. Ask yourself if this is an: introductory call, probing call, follow up call, simple demonstration, or a full-blown complex presentation? Allot the proper amount of time for that level of presentation and inform your client as well during the appointment call.

Don't assume that certain times are not available for customer contact. You can easily talk yourself out of the workweek by assuming certain times are unavailable for customer contact. Some common misconceptions: Monday morning, any weekday before 9 AM, after 3:30 PM, lunch hour, and after 2:30 on Friday afternoon. All of these times are viable if the customer wants to see you then.

Helpful Hints: Always have a call purpose or goal in mind when you call for an appointment or go a sales call. Be able to articulate that goal to yourself and your sales manager, or else, don't go! Align your calls with the company vision.

Be careful not to become a "star salesperson" by scheduling yourself in all four corners of your territory in the same day. Try to work in one geographical area to minimize driving time and maximize customer contact time.

Reporting

It will be rare if you do not have some level of activity and results reporting package that must be turned in to your supervisor. Your employer will typically supply the forms and deadlines for your reports. Some common reports are:

1. Expense reports (Do not be surprised, salespeople often charge or spend their personal money and are reimbursed later)
2. Monthly planning in advance
3. Weekly call reports (Similar to the form used on the previous page)
4. Annual plan

5. Monthly territory recap in writing

Monthly reports may include the following categories:

1. Significant account activities
2. Financial summary – Sales/Gross Profit
3. 30 to 90-day forecast
4. Competitor Activity – Pricing, account penetration, marketing/sales activity, new products
5. Large pending business/Large orders booked & shipped
6. Problems/Concerns – Product quality, lack of product, customer service levels
7. People on the move – clients, competitors, suppliers, distributors
8. For Managers – New hires, training provided, marketing initiatives, achievements, staff report

Summary

The reporting package serves two purposes. First it allows your management to gain insight into your time usage, account contacts and products presented. For the salesperson, it forces you to pre-plan and demands a degree of accountability that your employer has every right to expect. In addition, it is an extra tool that prompts you to follow up with prospects and supply them with the information they need to purchase your product.

13. Ethics

As you reflect on the relationship you have with your professional service people (Doctors, CPA's, Lawyers), and local retail merchants (Food, cleaners, clothing, hardware, plumbers, etc.) there is some element of trust that you place in their ability to deliver a quality product. What is it about their conduct that promotes that trust?

The same issues confront you as a representative of your employer in a highly competitive marketplace. The trust you build will be reflected not only in long term good will, but also in the sales level you are able to achieve. This trust and resulting reputation is a direct result of you and your company practicing the truth.

The truth can be practiced in many different ways. Let's examine a few of the ways that truth can be practiced by listing some proper conduct versus improper conduct.

Proper Conduct			Improper Conduct	
Tell Truth-Product & Capabilities			1/2 truths & lies	
Stand behind warranty			Warranty default	
Valid marketing claims			Unbelievable claims	
Arrive on time			Constantly tardy	
Accurate statement			Inaccurate claims	
Concerning competition/truthfulness			Slandering your competitor	
Accurate expense reporting			False expense reports	
Accurate call reports			Falsified call reports	
Timely product delivery			Late product delivery	
Ship correct product			Ship substitutes	
Accurate invoices			Purposeful inaccuracies	
Trustworthy service			Exaggerated service claims	
Competitive pricing			Opportunistic pricing policy	
Clean, fair competitor			Bends the rules, gifts,	
			lavish entertainment, &	
			kickbacks	

Ethics affect all individuals – from the financial clerk to the high-level executive. Individuals make daily decisions based on their individual values. Some companies and professional organizations have formulated a code of ethics as a statement of aspirations and a standard of integrity beyond that required by law.

The list below is ten essential values that should be considered as central to relations between people.

1. Caring
2. Honesty
3. Accountability

4. Promise keeping
5. Pursuit of excellence
6. Loyalty
7. Fairness
8. Integrity
9. Respect for others
10. Responsible citizenship

A Seven Step Decision Model for Ethical Issues

1. Determine the facts – what, who, where, when, how
2. Define the ethical issues (includes identifying the identifiable parties affected by the decision made or action taken)
3. Identify major principles, rules and values
4. Specify the alternatives
5. Compare norms, principles, and values with alternatives to see if a clear decision can be reached.
6. Assess the consequences
7. Make your decision

Certainly, these comments and this list are far from comprehensive. However, the point is made that improper conduct can lead everywhere from a temporary loss of business to the most catastrophic results imaginable. From the loss of your job, reputation, up to and including fines and jail sentences. The gain is nowhere remotely worth the risk. Not to mention, this conduct is simply wrong. Regardless of the number of people fudging on reports or product quality, it never justifies your participation.

14. Summary

This material is meant to be an introduction to the basic skill sets needed to begin one's career in sales or simply a review of the basics for someone needing a refresher course.

Some higher-level skills were not addressed. For the newcomer, an introduction provides a significant challenge without expecting them to master the higher-level skills necessary in major national accounts or intense negotiations.

A quick review reveals that every aspect of preparation, presentation, closing, and territory management was discussed in sufficient detail to increase the newcomer's knowledge level and skill.

This material can be self-administered, used in conjunction with a peer or sales manager, or taught as a two-day course by a Trucon Consulting Group instructor.

This material is a tried and proven template that will promote success if used diligently. No amount of training or coaching will guarantee success if the individual fails to strenuously apply themselves. Likewise, if the customer sector falls on difficult economic times or the employer fails to stay in a competitive position with up to date products and competitive pricing, will sales training ensure success.

However, without the proper training it is almost guaranteed that results will come much slower and be significantly more difficult for the entry level sales representative. The very nature of sales work makes it a difficult career path for many people. To receive the amount of rejection an average salesperson gets can be punishing to the newcomer. Therefore, the employer owes it to themselves and their sales associates to provide the level of training necessary to be competitive and win in their marketplace. This training fits that criteria extremely well.

Trucon's goal is to provide short, concise discourses and exercises to help the new associate learn the fundamentals well enough to out-plan and outsell their competitors. With enough discipline, study and repetition the new associate can master skills that will provide them with a lifetime of tremendous rewards in the selling field.

Solution Selling – A Different Selling Perspective

The previous sales instruction section advocates a probing question process to identify the prospect's real needs. Once those needs are identified, then the salesperson is tasked to present the product to the prospect so they will decide to purchase.

This process makes a major assumption. It assumes that the prospect has enough trust and interest to answer all those questions. This can be an issue due to the reticence of new prospects answering questions from a relative stranger. If you are in the early stages of developing awareness and interest in your product, then the deep question mode has inherent difficulties.

A solution selling perspective must rely on the marketing activities of the company to uncover viable prospects and quality them regarding the authority to make a purchasing decision. By necessity, if you have a small firm, then many of the marketing responsibilities will fall back on the owner or salesperson. Never-the-less it will always remain imperative to focus on your target market audience and qualify them before there is too much sunk cost in a non-viable potential customer.

The changes in the marketplace driven by the information available on the internet and the willingness of your prospect to do a deep level of research have made a solution selling strategy viable and necessary in many cases.

Your prospects are looking for real solutions that solve problems. That's why I have stressed the importance of the salesperson becoming a subject matter expert in the past.

In this case, it not simply just the salesperson, but the entire company that must be willing to offer a package of customized, bundled products and services to solve issues and earn business.

One of the distinct keys to having success with this approach is retaining salespeople who are schooled and experienced enough in the target market industry to be able to interact as a true resource to their prospects.

They should be able to put a unique proposal together that gives the prospect a new way to manage or approach their business. As a salesperson, they should be so knowledgeable about the prospect's business that it serves as a foundation that allows them to make firm recommendations to the prospect's staff and methods of doing business.

The salesperson should know what the real market drivers are for that industry. For example, in the crude oil marketplace in the domestic United States, $60 a barrel represents a benchmark of profitability that will allow a drilling company and producer to pay for the drilling, production and transportation costs and still make a viable profit. In contrast, crude oil produced in Saudi Arabia requires a higher cost per barrel price due to the commitment to the extensive royal family to provide living subsidies. This market data is available on a daily basis.

The Solution Selling method may entail having the salesperson teach the prospect's staff and production people about how their product will make them more competitive in the marketplace. Which is essentially another aspect of making the salesperson a subject matter expert.

As an engaged sales agent in the process, this strategy will challenge you to provide alternatives and act as an ongoing consultant. Make sure that as the representative for the supplier company you are in communication with every department in the company where your solution will have an impact.

All of these strong capabilities will allow you to challenge the prospect to make a purchasing and implementation decision.

The author has seen this method work very well in the semiconductor production tool and wafer manufacturing business. The strongest supplier in the static control and static induced contamination control market dominated the minds and purchasing decisions of the major players in the semi market due to PhD level research, publications, association participation and highly knowledgeable system of direct representatives and well-respected rep firms. They challenged the semiconductor contamination staff at the manufacturers with research from their own labs that exceeded the research at the manufacturer's people. And they dominated the market!

These brief comments provide an outline of the thought processes necessary to stepping in with a business solution proposal. To implement these changes may require some deep training or attracting people from your target market that can provide you with the expertise necessary to deliver real solution selling alternatives. Be careful that you don't allow this perspective to be ignored. It could be a vein of pure gold for your company.

Working it Backward
Your Mandatory Activity

This information relates to the sales and marketing checklist found on page 133 in this book. This discussion assumes that you have little or no repeat business. It is not for the sales professional who has established accounts producing business on a monthly basis.

This article assumes that you as a salesperson must proactively engage with enough prospects to meet or exceed your goal.

The first number that must be identified is your close rate. If you are new in your industry, then use the close rate for your company and industry. We are going to assume for the purposes of this discussion that your close rate is 25%.

Once you have this historical figure in mind it will be necessary for you to qualify your prospects probability of making a purchase. Consider the length of time that it may take based on the prospect's feedback about the budget year, the strength of demand for your product and the money available for that acquisition. Place a probability percentage on each potential close.

This is a good time to recommend a separate close list for all your prospects on one single spread sheet. I like using a color-coded Excel spread sheet with update notes for this purpose outside of my CRM.

Sample Close List

Company	Contact	Product	Note	Follow Up	Close %
ATX Machine	Fred Jones	Training	$1000 Potential	Feb. 1st	66%
Insurance Broker	Randy Frye	LinkedIn Mining	$800 Month	Jan. 20	80%
DMA Services	George Smith	Full Sales Analysis	$3,500	Feb. 12	90%

Another important factor to be considered is the length of time from the first exchange of information until you actually close the business. Some low-ticket items may close in a week or less, while other products with higher prices and more complex technology can take several years to close. This has been labeled as the lead and lag process. This simply refers to the time when you start a marketing effort compared to when you capture business from that effort.

It has been reported by multiple sales research groups and verified by me that even a simple exchange of information can take ten to twelve attempts to connect before you can have a substantive conversation. This takes time and persistence to see this process through. Don't be surprised for this process to take eight to twelve weeks. Be careful not to deluge your prospect with phone calls and multiple texts and e-mails. Spaced repetition is a very practical way to approach your attempted contacts. Also take into consideration what you have been told by your prospect concerning their schedule and availability to talk.

The chart below will give you an idea of how a salesperson might proceed with a post meeting follow up process.

I hesitate to call this process as being purely a numbers game. As you can well see there are a number of other factors built into the sales and marketing process. For example, it is pure sales insanity to not have a target market identified. However, for the sake of clarity and as an example we will assume that all of these important characteristics of the sales approach have been taken into consideration.

For this example's sake let's assume that your goal is $100,000 a month or $1,200,000 a year. Your typical sale of a business-oriented software is $28,000 each.

Therefore, your goal is 43 units for the year. ($28,000 x 43 = $1,204,000.)

Since your close rate is 25%, then we now know that you need to make 172 highly qualified presentations during the year. Sounds pretty daunting doesn't it?

However, let's break it down into more bite size pieces.

173 quality meetings divided by 12 months means that you need 14.4 meetings per month. Let's round that up to 15!

15 quality meeting divided by 4 weeks equals 3.75 or 4 quality meeting per week. Now it's beginning to sound a little more achievable.

However, least I not be accused of being impractical, let's subtract some time from our equations. Let's assume you take a two-week vacation, take the normal USA holidays, (8 to 11 days), have training (3-5 days) and you miss 4 days during the year to take care of personal business or you are sick. This means you essentially have eleven months to hit your plan.

This means you need 16 quality meetings a month or 4 per week.

Once you grasp these numbers, it becomes very clear how valuable your time is. In addition, it is evident that your company, or your company and you have a very solid lead generating program active and in place. It is important to take advantage of the digital media tools available to you and your associates skill sets to help you achieve your plan.

I'm sure that you can take your individual situation and compute the numbers required to hit the assigned goals for the year.

Sales and Marketing Log and Check List

Small Medium Business Enterprise Assumption

It is wise idea to set benchmarks for your sales and marketing plans that allow you to chronicle your "Lead Generating Activities." This is labeled as Lead and Lag documentation. If you document your activities in a CRM that should allow you to generate a report that can be transferred to a chart that might resemble the one below.

Hold yourself accountable and celebrate when you accomplish your goals. Especially the goal of closed business!

Habits turn into natural rhythms. Once you have established a habit it becomes much easier. If your lead generating activities aren't yielding business, evaluate and change your activities if necessary.

Weekly Sales and Marketing Checklist

Category	Time	Amount	Accomplished
Weekly Newsletter Vertical #1	Weekly	1	
Weekly Newsletter Vertical #2	Weekly	1	
Weekly Newsletter Vertical #3	Weekly	1	
Social Media Posts	Weekly	4-8	
Outbound Phone Calls – Contact and Follow Up	Weekly	25	
One Minute Video in LinkedIn, Twitter, Facebook, Google Home Page – Your Expertise Area	Weekly (Tues, Wed, Thur)	3	
Networking Group Attendance	Weekly	3	
Personal Meetings One to One's or Product Presentations	Weekly	3-5	
Group Speech – Your Market Expertise	Monthly	1	
Newsletter creation, posting, blog writing	4 to 6 Hours A Week	Monitor and Log Results	

Communication / Persuasion

As salespeople and sales managers, we all tend to place a lot of emphasis on product knowledge. Then our tendency is to bash our prospects over their head with everything we know in an effort to impress them and close business.

I urge you **NOT** to do this. Carmine Gallo is a previous CNN anchor and publisher of eight books on communication; Gallo says we need to practice the **Rule of Three**. Cognitive researchers report that the human brain starts to feel an overload when presented with too much information at the same time.

Too help our prospects retain what we tell them we need to give them new information they have not heard before. We need to relay that information in the form of a story and tell it with a passion. Then we include three benefits in our story. **The Rule of Three** works.

Believe me, it works.

When I was growing up the Superman TV series opened by saying Superman was faster than a speeding bullet, more powerful than a train locomotive and that he could leap tall buildings with a single bound. Decades later, I still remember those three bullet points!

Communication tools are a critical skill set when we are tasked with connecting with our prospects. By the time most of the sales team actually engages with a prospect, they have done a significant amount of research on our product and company. This is not the time to "wing it."

I recently saw a job description for a technical sales position that listed "A gregarious, engaging personality" as one of the qualifiers for the position.

Smart Move!

As a salesperson one of our first goals is to establish a trust connection with your prospect. This bond is one of the psychological triggers that helps move the sale closer to a close. Of course, we must never forget that product knowledge is a foundation, however connecting by being personable, open and positive starts to set the tone.

Find something in common with your prospect and of course work to communicate that you have their best interests in mind. Share stories because people remember stories and it relaxes the dynamic tension that often exists between a customer and salesperson. There must be no hint of arrogance in your demeanor.

I also highly recommend that you develop a working knowledge of the **DISC personality profile** and use that knowledge to approach your customer in the most effective manner. Work on using these methods and notice the cooperation and trust soar in your selling relationships.

And **never forget that integrity is your best long-term selling tool,** that can help keep a continuous pipeline of business coming your way for years to come.

In this buying and selling world that we all exist, it is better to communicate clearly and persuasively than to create animosity with our choice of words.

You may ask; how can persuasiveness be considered a business principle to be followed? It must be considered a principle because the choice of words and proper delivery of these words can build a relationship, seal an agreement and open doors for further discussion. Therefore, persuasiveness becomes an absolute necessity for those untold millions in the field of selling products.

There are ways to present your position without offending someone's intelligence. In fact, you can make your proposal quite appealing to those who may require your products.

There are a couple of basic requirements to good quality communication. The first one is to know the other individual's level of knowledge in the area you are talking about. The second is to understand their level of need. Then, you must take your product or proposal knowledge and present it in such a manner that it is appealing and clearly communicates how it will fill their needs.

Be aware that the first response will often be rejection or indifference if you have not established credibility with your prospect. Some level of trust must be established before a meaningful conversation can proceed. That trust can be created with your company's capability documentation, well written product literature, annual reports, third party references and the communicator's verbal presentation skills and appearance.

Presentation skills can be demonstrated by using the proper technical terms to precisely communicate the benefits of your product. The use of powerful words is necessary. Terms like confidence, reliable, long-term, return-on-investment, leading technology, rock solid, sought after and quality, are a few terms that promote confidence in your offering.

Avoid weak words like: I hope, I guess, maybe, probably, iffy, unproven and experimental. I am not recommending untruthful statements, just declarations emphasizing the benefits to the customer.

It is common to have your marketing department write feature and benefit statements for your products. Then determine what the exact needs of your clients are and present these statements to answer their concerns.

Avoid the hype and exaggeration that turns off many prospects. Then confidently proceed to describe why your product should be chosen over your competitors. Avoid the emotional involvement that leads to anger and rash statements judging your prospects intelligence and wisdom. Keep in mind that emotional outbursts frequently lead to lost business.

Be aware that people make decisions based on both emotional and logical evaluation criteria. If you can determine how to help your prospect avoid personal embarrassment, loss, or a hurt to someone or something they care deeply about, then part of the emotional persuasion process is solved. Or if you can help them promote the cause of a deeply emotional issue, then a large part of the emotional selling is also completed.

Remember that businesspeople are judged on the quality of the vendors they select. A poor choice reflects poorly on them, just as an outstanding choice makes them look like a savvy professional.

I personally take great encouragement and satisfaction when I sense a bond of trust developing due to the ability to describe a product with accurate, honest and persuasive language. The ability to differentiate your position with a clear description provides a winning ability that pays off personally and professionally for many years.

Successful Negotiations Skills

**Gary D. Seale: MBA - Principal
Trucon Sales Consulting
Austin, TX**

Successful Negotiations Skills
Contents

Successful Negotiations Skills

Session One

1. When Not to Propose a Negotiation

A. When the sales process is not complete

B. It is difficult to negotiate when the product you are providing is a commodity. Reason: Pricing is almost totally dictated by the market. However, if other services can be wrapped around the commodity, then the negotiating process can be undertaken. Example: Industrial on-site store providing a commodity but providing additional services. Or, as a distributor having some exclusive lines in your product mix.

C. It is not necessary to negotiate when you have an existing high trust relationship.

Participant questions:

- Does your company provide goods or services in a commodity market?

- If yes, can you differentiate your commodity with offsetting benefits?

2. Steps in the Selling Process

It is important to understand the difference between the selling process and negotiation. Negotiation should take place after all attempts have been made to overcome objections raised during the selling process. To launch into premature negotiating is a mistake that will cause confusion and cost you profit dollars. Please review the steps listed below and be aware that <u>negotiation will only be appropriate after step number five</u>.

1. Prospecting
2. Preparation
3. Probing and Presentation
4. Overcoming Objections
5. Obtaining Commitment
6. Building a Long-Term Relationship

- **Overcoming objections exercise in class – See the instructor for specific instructions**

<u>Important Tip</u>

Both parties must be open to the negotiation. It should be perfectly clear to each company what they are involved in. The sales process is over, the seller has a tentative commitment, however there is a point or several points that must be agreed upon.

Don't be surprised at objections, they should be expected as a normal part of the selling process.

3. Set an Agenda

A. Choose a team of diverse internal and external team members
B. Appoint a spokesperson - Not an individual with final authority
C. Keep the team small - 3-4 members maximum
D. Why - To establish clarity, structure and a positive environment
E. How – Summarize the situation to date, detail and confirm the objections
F. Determine a time, time duration and place

Participant Questions / Exercise:

In your existing organization, name two team members and a spokesperson as if you were going to engage in a negotiation.

Name at least one outside advisor that you would like to have involved:

4. Everything is Negotiable

- In a negotiation every concession must be accompanied by an offsetting trade. The tradeoff does not have to be of equal value. There may be an emotional need met that the other party values over money or material items.

- Why does there have to be a tradeoff for every concession until the final agreement is reached? Because we start with the maximum request and the truth demands a tradeoff; or in essence we lied when we made our first offer.

- Do not settle individual points of concern until all the points are discussed and a final settlement is pending.

5. Critical Pre-Positioning

- Develop an "ultimate goal." There will be a higher probability you will achieve more of your goals. In other words, set high expectations which become benchmarks for this and future negotiations.

- Do **NOT** under any circumstances artificially inflate your first offer simply because you know a concession will be expected.
- Ask for the maximum, then come down if you must. This is not false negotiating. The high standard is what you would truly like to achieve, not an arbitrary criterion set to start the negotiation.
- A sales team should start with the maximum quality and price.
- Buyers ask for the maximum in price reductions and concessions
- Have options:

*** Critical Pre-Positioning Work ***

A. **Maximum**: A truthful but high position
B. **Interim**: A position between maximum and acceptable
C. **Acceptable**: Becomes the last tenable position
D. **Walk Away**: Unacceptable - Setting poor precedents or possible money loss

An example of a tiered pricing and serving plan follows. Placing a level of services in conjunction with tiered pricing in writing helps the other party understand that effort levels and pricing are quantifiable. A written document gives your position credibility.

Sales Services Proposal

Outbound sales programs can be customized to meet individual client's requirements. However, a typical program provided by Trucon will include the following components:

* Obtain the required product knowledge to be conversant - Client to provide information

* Develop a call script - Joint Development

* Develop an e-mail follow up piece introducing the service - Joint development

* Obtain or develop Pdfs / Jpegs to send with follow up e-mail - Client/Trucon Provided

* Trucon supplies prospect list in client's specified demographic profile

* All calls and follow ups logged into an ACT CRM system

* Client receives immediate notice of appointment agreement or desire for more details

* Client receives weekly call report with record of responses
* Pre-qualified, experienced sales associates will make the calls

* Agreement governed by contract - 6 months with 30 day written break notice

Pricing is in tiers reflecting the number of outbound calls and follow-ups desired by the client.

Tier One:	$900	300 Calls
Tier Two:	$1,725	650 Calls
Tier Three:	$2,300	925 Calls

* Call volume includes initial calls, follow-ups, e-mail follow-ups, attempt volume varies due to length of calls, individual account research, and follow up with Trucon client on the hand off

These tiers constitute a true sales program. Product knowledge and selling skills are required of every

Trucon associate. Records are created for each attempt to contact; prospects are placed in a follow up / sales pipeline if they are not inclined to buy on a short-term basis. Accountability is achieved by a weekly reporting program. Competitive marketing information is gathered.

A prospect database is created that becomes the client's property.

Student Exercise

Select one of your primary product offerings and develop a maximum offer, an acceptable position and a walk away position. Use at least two variables in your exercise.

You may be pleasantly surprised at the concessions you can receive once the other party understands that you are prepared to walk-away if certain conditions are not met. This writer has seen this firm position strategy work in real estate, automobiles, retail, industrial sales and in services. It is preferable to earn the business by quality and competitive pricing; however, this strategy can be used in a very diplomatic way. The other party must fully understand why business cannot be conducted in any other way. It does take a high and very honest level of communication to use this strategy effectively.

Example

XYZ Widgets Co.	Price	Units	Delivery
Maximum	$5	10,000	6 WKS ARO
Interim	$4.???	< 10,000 > 6,000	4 WKS ARO
Acceptable	$4.35	6,000	3 WKS ARO
Walk-Away	$3.75	5,000	< 3WKS ARO

- ARO = After Receipt of Order

- All three items do not have to decline together, but you now have the options to create a trade-off
- If you unilaterally concede, then it's a gift or you are perceived as having started artificially high
- When the other party clearly understands the ground rules, then the process will not seem unrealistic or underhanded
- Your first concession will be your largest one, everything thereafter is in much smaller increments

6. Confirm All Objections

- Know all the customer's objections. If you don't, you may alter your proposal then discover later that other objections make your new proposal unworkable or unprofitable. Do not allow the customer to piecemeal the deal line-by-line. Listen intently and ask probing questions.

- As an example: A CPA has entered a negotiation for ongoing accounting services with a small manufacturer. They agree that $2,000 a month is a fair exchange for the services required. The CPA assumes that he will work at will, for time he calculates that the work will demand. However, the company owner then demands that the CPA be onsite for 30 hours a week. The CPA has set himself up for a confrontation or impasse by agreeing to a condition on a piecemeal basis.

7. Examine the Alternatives

- Why – To clarify all the customer needs
- Test alternatives....What if? – General ideas and specific alternatives
- Invite customer input
- Stress the benefits
- Make it look difficult
- Confirm agreement with the customer

The alternatives that you have available are going to be determined by the aspects of your industry and company. The latitude that you exercise will be a condition of how much power you have been granted in the negotiation. Remember it is a good idea to have somewhat limited power and to keep your negotiating team small and nimble.

The list that follows should give you a representative example from the alternatives available to businesses in general. Be sure to carefully research and brainstorm every avenue of latitude you might use in the interchange.

Alternatives List

- Packaging and delivery quantities
- Freight rates
- Labor rates
- Length of the contract
- Contract renewal criteria
- Early contract termination penalties
- Hold harmless agreements
- Quality of the product or service delivered
- Service times
- Length of the service support
- Quantity and price breaks
- Product and professional service pricing
- Firm pricing commitment - (Length of time)
- Delivery times
- Post-delivery training
- Commissions percentages
- Pay backs on commissions
- Policy coverage

- Deductibles ($'s)
- Communication criteria (Ex: Advance notice of material change)
- Accounts payable
- Prompt payment discounts
- Non-tangible tradeoff items Example: Titles, referrals
- Safety stock held for client
- Brand specifications (No substitutes)
- Penalty clauses - legal action (Failure to complete deliverables)
- Non-compete agreements
- Non-disclosure agreements

8. Take Bold Initiatives

- Boldness is a personal and business judgment
- Float up some trial balloons - Make a generalized position statement (Example: That's way out in left field, you're out of my box, that dog won't hunt, Ouch! You're hurting me now.)
- Negotiate all the differences until all are under agreement
- Maximize profit or savings.
- Develop multiple options and be imaginative.

Example:

Determining a price will be a function of competition, product cost, turns, cash flow, market strategies, cost of operations, required profits and a number of other company and personal criteria. All of these factors must be taken into consideration when using price as a bargaining tool. Be careful not to set harmful precedents that will damage profitability in other business units, geographic areas and in the future.

Student Exercise:

Discuss the tactic of "Crunching" as presented by the instructor. (Crunching is a bold exaggeration meant to catch everyone's attention)

1. **Is it a tactic you would use?**
2. **Who would it be appropriate with?**
3. **Why would you use it?**
4. **Do you consider it professional?**
5. **Discuss the possibility of a crunching tactic killing the negotiation.**

Session One Conclusion

Session one lays the foundation for every aspect of your potential negotiation. Be sure that you understand:

1. When not to negotiate
2. That the sales process must be completed before you start negotiating
3. Set the stage for your negotiation by clarifying that everything is negotiable
4. Preplan your four criteria for the negotiation beforehand
5. Develop as many options as feasible and be bold

Session Two

9. Primary Motivating Factors

One preliminary item that the negotiator should have some knowledge about is: What motivates people? This topic could easily become a completely separate training class with volumes of information. However, some knowledge of basic motivational factors should be helpful as you read and study this material. Four very basic motivating factors have been categorized as:

- Fear: Described as the punitive effects of nature or others as a consequence of your actions or non-action. An example might be jail time and heavy fines as a result of some criminal activity. Or perhaps the fear of falling. Fear of lost reputation is a good example.

- Hate: Revenge, slander, libel, avoidance, anger, depression, apathy, to detest. A very strong, often short-term motivating force that influences some to severe actions or strong performances. Righteous - justifiable anger

- Love: (A JUST cause) The type of extremely deep concern that allows a person to substitute their interests for the needs of another. An example might be that of a mother for her infant child.

- Control: The desire and or ability to control other people or organizations. Ego, power, arrogance.

These motivating factors provide someone with the power to act or exert influence over another person. If you can give someone something that they desire, you can have power over that person. The other party has to grant you that power. Some examples: The buyer/seller relationship, parent/child relationship, manager/subordinate relationship. You can also have power if you are able to withhold something that someone desires.

Webster's' Dictionary states that power is: The capacity to exert force, to act with force or vigor. The ability to control others through authority or influence.

People also have needs that become motives for their actions. People need:

1. Security: Food, water, shelter, clothing, be free from threat

2. Significance: Identification with a group – Family, work, social, educational. Ego – talent, abilities and achievements

3. Identity – Close to significance – In our culture it is closely tied to occupation, beliefs, or actions, religious or political identities, or family roles

Why is the knowledge of the motivating forces and needs of the other party important? It tells us how and why they are going to pursue their goals.

DISC Profile

To assist with the understanding of yourself, your associates and the individuals you may be negotiating with, it is highly recommended that you step outside this training session and take a DISC test. The DISC is a commonly used personality profile that provides deep insight into our strong inclinations for action and how we perceive the world and those in it.

DISC stands for the propensity to be Dominating, an Influencer, a Steady person or someone concerned with Compliance.

One excellent test provided online is from the Tony Robbins organization and can be accessed at the website below.

http://www.tonyrobbins.com/ue/disc-profile.php

Review your DISC profile and now read what to expect and how to deal with other people with the four primary characteristics in your negotiating session.

I. Understanding and Working with People

The assessments classify four aspects of behavior by testing a person's preferences in word associations. DISC is an acronym for:

- **D**ominance – relating to control, power and assertiveness
- **I**nfluence – relating to social situations and communication
- **S**teadiness – relating to patience, persistence, and thoughtfulness
- **C**ompliance (or caution) – relating to structure and organization

Dominance: People who score high in the intensity of the "D" styles factor are very active in dealing with problems and challenges, while low "D" scores are people who want to do more research before committing to a decision. High "D" people are described as demanding, forceful, egocentric, strong willed, driving, determined, ambitious, aggressive, and pioneering. Low D scores describe those who are conservative, low keyed, cooperative, calculating, undemanding, cautious, mild, agreeable, modest and peaceful.

Influence: People with high "I" scores influence others through talking and activity and tend to be emotional. They are described as convincing, magnetic, political, enthusiastic, persuasive, warm, demonstrative, trusting, and optimistic. Those with low "I" scores influence more by data and facts, and not with feelings. They are described as reflective, factual, calculating, skeptical, logical, suspicious, matter of fact, pessimistic, and critical.

Steadiness: People with high "S" styles scores want a steady pace, security, and do not like sudden change. High "S" individuals are calm, relaxed, patient, possessive, predictable, deliberate, stable, consistent, and tend to be unemotional and poker faced. Low "S" intensity scores are those who like change and variety. People with low "S" scores are described as restless, demonstrative, impatient, eager, or even impulsive.

Compliance: People with high "C" styles adhere to rules, regulations, and structure. They like to do quality work and do it right the first time. High "C" people are careful, cautious, exacting, neat, systematic, diplomatic, accurate, and tactful. Those with low "C" scores challenge the rules and want independence and are described as self-willed, stubborn, opinionated, unsystematic, arbitrary, and unconcerned with details.

D (Drive) Often called Type A's - Domineering

General Characteristics:

- Direct. Decisive. High Ego Strength. Problem Solver. Risk Taker. Self-Starter

Value to Team:

- Bottom-line organizer, cuts to the real issues rapidly. Places value on time. Challenges the status quo. Innovative

Possible Weaknesses:

- Oversteps authority. Argumentative attitude, especially with other D's. Dislikes routine. Attempts too much at once. Looks down on others not like them. Hurt feelings of others and are unaware they do so. Glosses over details.

Greatest Concern:

- Being taken advantage of – Losing face.

Motivated By:

- New challenges. Power and authority to take risks and make decisions. Freedom from routine and mundane tasks. Changing environments in which to work and play. Ego ride.

Ideal Environment:

- Innovative focus on future. Non-routine challenging tasks and activities. Projects that produce tangible results. Freedom from controls, supervision, and details. Personal evaluation based on results, not methods. Latitude with spending.

Remember a High D May Want:

- Authority, varied activities, prestige, freedom, assignments promoting growth, "bottom line" approach, and opportunity for advancement.

DO:

- Be brief, direct, and to the point. Ask "what" not "how" questions. Focus on business; remember they desire results. Suggest ways for him/her to achieve results, be in charge, and solve problems. Highlight logical benefits of featured ideas and approaches.

DON'T:

- Ramble. Repeat yourself. Focus on problems. Be too sociable. Make generalizations. Make statements without support.

While analyzing information, a High D may:

- Ignore potential risks. Not weigh the pros and cons. Not consider others' opinions. Offer innovative and progressive systems and ideas.

D's possess these positive characteristics in teams:

- Autocratic managers - great in crisis. Self-reliant. Innovative in getting results. Maintain focus on goals. Specific and direct. Overcome obstacles. Provide direction and leadership. Push group toward decisions. Willing to speak out. Generally optimistic. Welcome challenges without fear. Accept risks. See the big picture. Can handle multiple projects. Function well with heavy workloads.

Personal Growth Areas for D's:

- Strive to be an "active" listener. Be attentive to other team members' ideas until everyone reaches a consensus. Be less controlling and domineering. Develop a greater appreciation for the opinions, feelings, and desires of others. Put more energy into personal relationships. Show your support for other team members. Take time to explain the "whys" of your statements and proposals. Be friendlier and more approachable.

I (Influence) The life of the party – Sanguine – Happy Go Lucky

General Characteristics:

- Enthusiastic. Trusting; Optimistic. Persuasive; Talkative. Impulsive; Emotional, Scattered, appears to be frivolous

Value to Team:

- Creative problem solver. Great encourager. Motivates others to achieve. Positive sense of humor. Negotiates conflicts; peace maker.

Possible Weaknesses:

- More concerned with popularity than tangible results. Inattentive to detail. Overuses gestures and facial expressions. Tends to listen only when it's convenient.

Greatest Fear:

- Rejection.

Motivated By:

- Flattery, praise, popularity, and acceptance. A friendly environment. Freedom from many rules and regulations. Other people available to handle details.

Ideal Environment:

- Practical procedures. Few conflicts and arguments. Freedom from controls and details. A forum to express ideas. Group activities in professional and social environments

Remember a High I May Want:

- Social esteem and acceptance, freedom from details and control, people to talk to, positive working conditions, recognition for abilities, opportunity to motivate and influence others.

DO:

- Build a favorable, friendly environment. Give opportunity for them to verbalize about ideas, people and their intuition. Assist them in developing ways to transfer talk into action. Share testimonials from others relating to proposed ideas. Allow time for stimulating, sociable activities. Submit details in writing, but don't dwell on them. Develop a participative relationship. Create incentives for following through on tasks.

DON'T:

- Eliminate social time. Do all the talking. Ignore their ideas or accomplishments. Tell them what to do.

While analyzing information, a High I may:

- Lose concentration. Miss important facts and details. Interrupt. Be creative in problem solving.

I's possess these positive characteristics in teams:

- Instinctive communicators. Participative managers - influence and inspire. Motivate the team. Spontaneous and agreeable. Respond well to the unexpected. Create an atmosphere of wellbeing. Enthusiastic. Provide direction and leadership. Express ideas well. Work well with other people. Make good spokespersons. Will offer opinions. Persuasive. Have a positive attitude. Accomplish goals through people. Good sense of humor. Accepting of others. Strong in brainstorming sessions.

Personal Growth Areas for I's:

- Weigh the pros and cons before making a decision; be less impulsive. Be more results oriented. Exercise control over your actions, words, and emotions. Focus more on details and facts. Remember to slow down your pace for other team members. Talk less; listen more. Consider and evaluate ideas from other team members. Concentrate on following through with tasks.

S (Steadiness) The supporter – Phlegmatic – Quiet – Submissive – Low Key - But resolved

General Characteristics:

- Good listener; Team player. Possessive. Steady; Predictable. Understanding; Friendly.

Value to Team:

- Reliable and dependable. Loyal team worker. Compliant towards authority. Good listener, patient and empathetic. Good at reconciling conflicts.

Possible Weaknesses:

- Resists change. Takes a long time to adjust to change. Holds a grudge; sensitive to criticism. Difficulty establishing priorities.

Greatest Fear:

- Loss of security.

Motivated By:

- Recognition for loyalty and dependability. Safety and security. No sudden changes in procedure or lifestyle. Activities that can be started and finished.

Ideal Environment:

- Practical procedures and systems. Stability and predictability. Tasks that can be completed at one time. Few conflicts and arguments. A team atmosphere.

Remember a High S May Want:

- Security in situations, sincere appreciation, repeated work patterns, time to adjust to change, limited territory of responsibility.

DO:

- Create a favorable environment: personal and agreeable. Express a genuine interest in them as a person. Provide them with clarification for tasks and answers to "how" questions. Be patient in drawing out their goals. Present ideas or departures from current practices in a non-threatening manner; give them time to adjust. Clearly define goals, procedures and their role in the overall plan. Assure them of personal follow-up support. Explain how their actions will minimize the risks involved and enhance current procedures.

DON'T:

- Be pushy, overly aggressive, or demanding. Be too confrontational.

While analyzing information, a High S may:

- Be openly agreeable but inwardly unyielding. Internalize their concerns and doubts. Hesitate to share feedback during presentation. Slow down the action. Provide valuable support for team goals.

S's possess these positive characteristics in teams:

- Instinctive relaters. Participative managers - accomplish goals through personal relationships. Make others feel like they belong. Show sincerity. Can see an easier way of doing things. Focused and intuitive about people and relationships. Full of common sense. Buy into team goals. Dependable. Identify strongly with the team. Strive to build relationships. Provide stability. Consider elements of a total project. Realistic and practical. Even-tempered. Provide specialized skills. Show patience with others. Loyal.

Personal Growth Areas for S's:

- Be more open to change. Be more direct in your interactions. Focus on overall goals of the team rather than specific procedures. Deal with confrontation constructively. Develop more flexibility. Increase pace to accomplish goals. Show more initiative. Work at expressing thoughts, opinions, and feelings.

C (Compliance) The Perfectionist – Melancholy – Introverted – Moody – The Artist – Thinker

Engineer - Teacher

General Characteristics:

- Accurate; analytical. Conscientious; careful. Factfinder; precise. High standards; systematic.

Value to Team:

- Perspective: "the anchor of reality." Conscientious and even-tempered. Thorough to all activities. Defines situation; gathers, criticizes and tests information.

Possible Weaknesses:

- Needs clear-cut boundaries for actions/relationships. Bound by procedures

167

and methods. Gets bogged down in details. Prefers not to verbalize feelings. Will give in rather that argue.

Greatest Fear:

- Criticism.

Motivated By:

- Standards of high quality. Limited social interaction. Detailed tasks. Logical organization of information.

Ideal Environment:

- Tasks and projects that can be followed through to completion. Specialized or technical tasks. Practical work procedures and routines. Few conflicts and arguments. Instructions and reassurance that they are doing what is expected of them.

Remember a High C May Want:

- Autonomy and independence, controlled work environment, reassurance, precise expectations and goals, exact job descriptions, planned change.

DO:

- Prepare your case in advance. Delineate pros and cons of proposed ideas. Support ideas and statements with accurate data. Reassure them that no surprises will occur. Submit an exact job description with a precise explanation of how that task fits into the big picture. Review recommendations with them in a systematic and comprehensive manner. Be specific when agreeing. Disagree with the facts rather than the person when disagreeing. Be patient, persistent, and diplomatic while providing explanations.

DON'T:

- Refuse to explain details. Answer questions vaguely or casually.

While analyzing information, a High C may:

- Become overly cautious and conservative. Get too bogged down in details. Avoid or postpone decisions, especially if they perceive a risk. Be an effective trouble shooter.

C's possess these positive characteristics in teams:

- Instinctive organizers. "Do it yourself" managers - create and maintain systems. Strive for a logical, consistent environment. Control the details. Conscientious. Evaluate the team's progress. Ask important questions. Maintain focus on tasks. Offer conservative approaches. Emphasize quality. Think logically. Will share risks and responsibilities. Work systematically. Will strive for consensus. Diplomatic. Analyze obstacles.

Personal Growth Areas for C's:

- Concentrate on doing the right things, not just doing things right. Be less critical of others' ideas and methods. Respond more quickly to accomplish team goals. Strive to build relationships with other team members. Be more decisive. Focus less on facts and more on people. Take risks along with other team members.

10. Take Time for Discovery

Time is valuable. Take the time and effort to learn the other party's real wants, needs and constraints. Make sure that you understand your own company's vision, mission and constraints as well.

To the best of your ability, become a subject matter expert. What aspects or benefits reside within your company that provide a benefit? Something they may need or want? Example: Terms, credit, markets, prospect lists, R & D, product lines, purchasing power, engineering, reputation, distribution channels, etc, etc. Research the other party's history, financial status, culture, ownership, stated long term goals. Involve someone on your team that has a keen sense of personality style and test the other person to see how their style works in a business situation. Always keep in mind the four key pre-positions you have agreed upon. Some examples of the other party's wants, needs and constraints that may come into play are:

- Budget
- Delivery – Mfg. capacity, warehouse location and capacity
- Spare Parts
- Local service and availability
- Technical support
- Certifications from an outside authority
- Warranty
- Equipment options
- Insurance
- Performance bond
- Training
- Quality requirements
- Authorized distributor
- Past performance – References
- Financial stability
- Just In time systems
- On site inventory and services
- 24/7 service
- Repairs
- Detail of equipment specifications available
- Depth and breadth of product offering
- Catalogs

- MIS capabilities
- Product knowledge
- Foreign substance abuse policy
- EEOC compliance
- Minority vendor usage
- Small/large business

Probe and listen carefully for answers, inadvertent comments, signs of confusion, positions that are heavily stressed, omissions or body language that communicates a need that has not been formally communicated. The following section will provide more detail on how to discover the other party's true position.

Student Exercise

Summarize a 10k report. Discuss the needs and constraints you have discovered in the 10K that could be used in a negotiation.

11. How Do We Learn

A. Practice observation skills: Observe the other party's appearance, demeanor, preparation, understanding, position, office, reputation and confidence. Specifically look at their weight, haircut, clothing, personal hygiene, or whether they are arrogant, humble or friendly. Are they prepared with facts, figures, dates, trends, industry standards and technical knowledge?

What hobbies or personal interests do they reveal by the decoration of their office? Do they exhibit an understanding of the situation and the effects of the negotiation? What level of confidence do they portray? What level of respect are they given by their peers?

B. Research: The company web site, LinkedIn, Google, periodicals, company newspaper, annual report,10K, payment history, D & B report, products produced or service rendered, policy statements, surveys, contracts in force, industry trends, lawsuits, pending legislation, and macro/micro economics of their industry.

C. Use open and closed probing questions: Open: Answers the questions, Who? What? Why? Where? When? How? Example: What was your position when the downward trend began? Closed: A specific question leading to an option or a yes or no answer. Example:

Research Assignment:

Find a publicly traded company in your industry and go to their website. Look under the financial investment pull down and find the link to their 10K quarterly report. The managerial team must report potential threats to the viability of the company as well as the recent financial statements.

Find three issues that may impact you or the other party's negotiating stance or willingness to concede in a certain area.

12. People Reading Tips

The ability to read people's nonverbal communications is far from an exact science. However, the willingness to observe the conduct of the other individual or team of individuals and analyze their conduct is an important skill that should not be overlooked. The following tips should provide a starting point for those of you who have not given this area much study or credibility.

1. Bored: Head in hand, blank stare, leaning back, glancing at watch
2. Concerned-Apprehensive: Furrowed forehead and eyebrows, hand over face, extremely sensitive to comments or suggestions, self-focus
3. Read the eyes: Groggy - Not interested Inquisitive or irritated – Mildly Interested Alert, Angry or Pleased – Riveted
4. Mouth: Ends up – Agreement Ends down – Disagreement Straight –Jury Out
5. Body leaning forward, direct eye contact, determined look on face – Focused, Concerned and Eager
6. Body back, neutral expression, casual eye contact – Weak interest, looking for diversion

7. Voice: Stuttering, nervous, loses focus – Lack of confidence, under prepared, weak position, lacks commitment
8. Voice: Firm, convinced, in combination with strong eye contact equals confidence, experience, prepared and committed. (Watch for bluffers: Be prepared to expose with your knowledge)
9. Voice: Lecturing style, loud, badgering – Overconfidence (Watch for strong arm tactics)
10. Voice: Telegraphs what people are going to say or the validity of what they are saying.

- In the Toastmasters International speaking organization, members are taught to be total communicators. People only accomplish 20-25% of their communication by what is said and 75-80% of the communication is in the way it is delivered. Therefore, it is imperative that as effective negotiators, you learn the art of reading verbal and non-verbal clues to the real meaning of what is being stated.

13. What Gives You Power

1. The ability to influence and control through withholding or supplying the other party's wants and needs. In addition, sticking to your commitments.

2. For the seller, power comes from the attributes of your company, product and personal ability. Examples: Product, third party references, printed

policies and procedures, price lists, quote conditions, credit policy, history, delivery, price, financial stability, value added services, education, experience, reputation, title, verbal ability.

3. Seller: Remember the buyer's limitations, pressures and problems. Example: Delivery, production problems, management pressure, cost, acquisition cost, job performance. The seller's quote of the 90's, "The pain of poor performance will linger long after the sweetness of low price has faded."

- Buyers: Remember seller's limitations, pressures and problems. Examples: Competitors, overstock, turns, cash flow, lead times, lack of selection, commission driven pay plans, expenses, management pressure and ego.

Student Exercise:

Stop here and list four key aspects of your company or service that will give you power in a negotiation

Share your points with a training peer and ask for feedback

14. Use Persuasion

Seller: Impress the prospect with how much you want the business. (Not need)

Seller: Choice of proper words, voice tone, eye contact, and body language emphasizing <u>benefits to the customer</u>. Examples: Faster, easier, clean, cost savings, impressive, safer, more simple, efficient, effective high quality. You do not "sell them," you lead them to a purchasing decision. As a goal the salesperson should be efficient with things and effective with people.

Seller: Dresses professionally, supplies prompt quality responses, sincere thanks, quality presentations, is knowledgeable about the products offered and is able to use this knowledge properly.

Buyer: Let's seller know you have other options. Example: Loss of the order, financial gain or loss, continuing the relationship with other suppliers.

No matter how tempting to do otherwise, always, always tell the truth.

Feature, Advantage, Benefit: A Proven Method of Persuasion.

Stating the <u>feature</u>, the advantage to that <u>feature</u> and a benefit that <u>feature</u> delivers is a superior method of presenting your case or product. This is called the **FAB** method.

The reasons to use the fab method are:

> ➤ So the prospect will understand
> ➤ So the prospect will agree
> ➤ So the prospect will take action

A **feature** is something you can:

> ➤ See
> ➤ Touch
> ➤ Measure

It is expressed as a noun. Detailing a feature answers the question, "What is it?"

An Advantage is:

The advantage is a performance characteristic of the feature. It answers the question. What will the feature do?

The Benefit is:

A benefit is an asset characteristic expressed as a personalized value. It answers the question, what does the product do for my company or me? People make decisions based on both logical and emotional criteria. Therefore, there are two types of benefit statements.

Logical: Stated in dollar terms or some other quantifiable basis

Emotional: Stated in personal terms

The logical aspect of a benefit:

  ➢ Makes money
  ➢ Saves money
  ➢ Saves time
  ➢ Makes time available
  ➢ Increases productivity
  ➢ Improves quality

The emotional aspect of a benefit:

  ➢ Provides recognition
  ➢ Denotes achievement
  ➢ Provides Security
  ➢ Promotes personal profit
  ➢ Reduces Worry
  ➢ Provides personal pleasure
  ➢ Reduces the hassle factor

What can you FAB?

  ➢ Product
  ➢ Company
  ➢ Service
  ➢ Program
  ➢ Yourself

To determine which features to focus on, find out what motivates your prospect. Look at the "big picture." In other words, what national or global influences are taking place? How is your competition positioned? What do you know about the plant or the industry as a whole? What have you learned from other staff members at the customers facility?

Reasons to develop benefits.

> Answers the number one question: "What's in it for me?"
> Appeals to the prospect's individual needs, wants, concerns and future plans.
> Feature and advantages only – imply benefits.
> Features and advantages only – invite comparison.
> Benefits are reasons for agreeing.
> Benefits are reasons for **Buying.**

Exercise: Use your information or knowledge, now write four feature, advantage and benefit statements regarding one of your company's primary products.

FAB statements:

1.

2.

3.

4.

Write a personal features list. After you compile your features list, write three FAB statements about your capabilities.

Potential list profile:

> Education
> Honors
> Previous experience
> Achievements
> Communication skills
> Technical skills
> Analytical skills
> Creativity
> Persistence
> Maturity

Three personal FAB statements:

1.

2.

3.

End of Session Two

Key Points in Session Two

1. What motivates people
2. Take time for discovery
3. Ethics
4. 10K report contents
5. What gives you power
6. Using persuasion - The FAB method

Session Three

15. Build Long Term Relationships

The negotiating situation has a strong potential for a breakdown of the relationship. Be careful to use language, attitudes and tactics that maintain or possibly build the relationship. A continuation of the relationship is more important than domination. Keep the door open until all options have been explored. If you are not able to conduct business, end the negotiation on an amicable note. The future is unknown, future dialogue and opportunities may exist. Build the relationship on truth and integrity. Professional conduct is an absolute, no temper displays, no stunts, no hidden agendas and no traps.

Emotional Conduct to Avoid or Issues to Be Aware of:

1. Anger: Avoid absolute language, no matter how tempting. Angry negotiators make mistakes and errors. Anger interferes with your ability to be objective and process information. Do not allow the other party to bait you into anger. If you feel yourself "losing it" take a time out.
2. Threatening: It incites hostility or withdrawal by the other party. If in doubt about the other party's understanding, educate, do not threaten. Do not respond to a threat. Stay calm and stay the course.

3. An Impasse: Don't be overly concerned it's a natural part of the bargaining process. However, if you're close to your time deadline and you are convinced the other side is not bluffing, then there may be a real issue. If absolutely necessary, walk away with a feeling that both sides gave it their all and live to bargain again together another day.
4. Verbal Explosions: Here's the bitter pill for you type A's. Do not interrupt, disagree or debate. Relax and don't reply. After they are through making a fool of themselves, say "thanks for clarifying your position."
5. A Walkout: If the other side wants to walk out, let them know how much you want to conclude the business, but if they proceed, let them. Allow an appropriate amount of time to elapse and then contact them. Don't let it phase you. This action just may have been an act to see if you will flinch. Never unilaterally precipitate a walkout yourself.

16. Types of Negotiating Styles

Integrating - Interested parties confront the issue, identify the problem, generate and weigh alternative solutions, and select a solution.

Obliging – An obliging person neglects their own concern to satisfy the concern of the other party.

Plays down differences while emphasizing commonalties.

Dominating – High concern for self, low concern for others. I win, you lose. Also called forcing. Used when an unpopular solution must be implemented. Tends to breed resentment.

Avoiding – Passive withdrawal from the problem or active suppression of the issue. Appropriate for trivial issues when the cost of confrontation outweighs the benefits of resolving the conflict.

Compromising – Give and take approach. Used when parties have opposite goals or have equal power.

Student Exercise:

Write down three emotional pitfalls that could stall a negotiation based on this training and your experience.

1.

2.

3.

17. Know When to be Quiet

- Avoid Revealing Remarks. Example: Factory problems that have no impact on quality or delivery, budgetary constraints, delivery deadlines
- Probe, look for remarks that might reveal an acute weakness
- Be an accurate listener. Have a team meeting to review each session after it is concluded.

18. Remember the Other Party's Needs

- What did you discover – don't ignore it – use it
- There are many wants and needs – people make decisions based on emotional and logical reasons
- Consequently, avoid exclusive focus on either category, focus on revealed needs
- Remember the primary human motivators

19. Negotiating Tips

- Seller - Spend more time on benefits instead of price
- Buyer – Spend more time on price – more likely to win concession
- People do things to meet their needs, not yours
- Repetition drives your point home

- People remember the first and last things presented
- Most concessions are given in the last 20% of the negotiation
- Start with minor issues and lead to major ones.

20. Differences

- Differences develop over:
- Price
- Deliverables – i.e. value
- Terms and Conditions

Student Exercise:

Brainstorm two or three ways that you can counter a demand for a price concession with a service or term other than a price concession.

1.

2.

Share your conclusions with your peer group.

21. A Win for all Parties Involved

- The agreement should satisfy the important needs of the <u>customer</u>, the <u>salesperson</u> and the <u>sales organization</u>.
- It is not a win for the customer to get all they want, and the sales side loses to the point it can no longer honor the agreement.
- Salespeople win when they earn the order, and gain respect and trust. Get an opportunity to build a long-term relationship
- Sales organization wins when they earn an acceptable profit, agree to reasonable commitments, avoid adverse precedents

22. Formulate an Agreement

- WHY – To bring an end to the negotiation
- HOW – Make a new complete proposal, detail the benefits, identify steps for finalizing the agreement

23. Put the Agreement in Writing

- Treat the agreement like a contract
- Two competent parties of legal age
- An offer
- An acceptance
- For some exchange of value, i.e. money
- In sufficient detail to govern the agreement, signed by both parties.

Session Three Conclusion

Key Points in Session Three

1. Build Long-Term Relationships
2. DISC Personality Styles
3. Know When to be Quiet
4. Understanding Where Differences Develop
5. Contract Terms - Put the Agreement in Writing

Ethics

Practicing the Truth

Depending on someone who practices deceit with their communication gives cause for a deep distrust and disdain for that individual. The consequences for the liar and the victim are embarrassing and costly. The cost can be counted in more ways than one.

Take for example the salesperson that lies about the product's capabilities and the company's support services to earn business. Once the product arrives, the shortcoming's become evident. Lost production time, shoddy product production, missed deliveries, reduced pricing required, lost opportunities, substandard communication, critical information lost, and stressed employees attempting to deal with an inferior product are just a few of the consequences.

For the seller's side; expensive retrofitting, redesign and programming, lost business and future opportunities go hand-in-hand with the lies told to gain the order. And for the individual salesperson, the complete distrust and hate from both the customer and the employer for placing them in the ugly circumstances the lies produced.

The negative impact of lying can spread its havoc and ruin. To the executive suite, politicians, civil servants, unions, marketing organizations and even religious organizations.

Have you ever been personally burned by someone you trusted? That level of pain is not easily forgotten, is it? It's no small wonder that trust is hard to earn and easy to lose in our society. With so many people practicing a relative standard when it comes to the truth, trust becomes a rare element. It's a little more like, "buyer beware" in both corporate and personal relationships, which is truly a shame.

Contrast the distrust produced by lying with the person who practices the truth regardless of the circumstances and personal consequences. There is a breath of fresh air surrounding your dealings with someone who takes great care to be accurate, fair minded and truthful in their representation of products, services and personal responsibilities. Not only is the trust level high in these individuals, but the long-term consequences are beneficial for all the parties involved with them. New opportunities, continued business, open doors, additional responsibilities, reliability, and confidence flow to and from the truthful person.

Greed

Arrogance and pride are motivators that lead to deception and compromise. Compromise easily allows one to justify a lie that initially leads to more profit and honor than is truly deserved.

The micro aspect of this concern is individual cheating from employers that rob the company of profit and productivity. Certainly, many images can be recalled from the press, individual experiences and personal temptations. Forgery on expense accounts, presenting a false front of due diligence, outright theft and lying to cover up deficiencies in ones efforts are all signs of greed.

I was able to witness firsthand an example of greed and theft in my first post college job. I was placed in a year-long management training course which required me to work in every department of an oil field drilling supply company.

Several trusted employees from the Special Quotations Department developed a company of their own, selling drilling equipment from the stock of our employer. They were working the sales side of the business while a long-term warehouse employee pilfered the inventory at night. After a secret investigation by the Texas Department of Public Safety, all the employees involved were dismissed from their jobs. They were very fortunate not to have criminal charges pressed against them. I knew one of the men involved very well, since we had volunteered to work with Junior Achievement together. He was the last guy on earth you would have suspected.

Rarely does a fraudulent activity go unnoticed for a long period of time. The consequences are not only physical penalties, but also the mental, emotional, and spiritual anguish associated with the misconduct.

The opposite spectrum of rank and file greed involves the systematic decisions of the senior management from large corporations. Even though there is consumer fraud in some industries, most of my previous employers were serious about supplying quality products and services. This reference is to be growing the profitability of the company by pushing employee productivity without rewarding the associates when additional growth and profits are realized. It has been documented in various business publications for the last decade that the percentage of profit growth has been achieved by associate productivity gains and holding wage increases well below those gains' percentage wise.

The leverage applied to senior management by the stockholders, the board of directors and management compensation packages to grow profitability leads to a greed strategy that penalizes thousands of trusting, hardworking employees.

Despite the pressures to capitulate and let greed be your motivation, businesspeople must look to the best long-term interest of all the stakeholders involved. The bond of trust that holds our free market enterprise system together can only be expected to last as long as all the parties involved act in the best interests of everyone involved. Laws, rules and regulations are a weak substitute for the ethical, other centered principles that should drive a successful enterprise.

Personal Character

Why is it these days that consistent character seems to be so woefully lacking in business practices?

Is it the highly competitive global economy?
Is it the acceptance of relativism?
Is it the proliferation of information available?
Is it the change in our educational systems?
Is it a win at any cost mentality?
Is it the pressure on profit margins?
Have political, sports, business and religious leaders set a bad example?

<u>Or, are all these things symptoms of an underlying deficiency in our thinking?</u>

Ultimately, a failure to accept the premises of honesty, purity, truthfulness, trustworthiness, excellence and service lead to inconsistent character qualities in individuals and companies.

Weak personal character traits are evidenced by lying, tardiness, falsified reports, missed assignments, and sloppy work. On a slightly larger scale they become failing to honor warranties, theft, false advertising or shuffling deliveries to satisfy the most demanding customer. On a macro scale, they become selling faulty products, fraud, padding corporate income statements and insider trading. There are a multitude of other overt actions that indicate a lack of integrity and commitment in the marketplace. Pick up your daily paper and you can commonly see some version of character failure spelled out on those pages.

The cost of poor character is made up of lost opportunities, distrust, lawsuits, prison time, demotions, terminations, shame, disgust and disappointment. These character failures also permeate the workplace and hurt innocent people who have far less of a golden parachute than the wealthy leaders who lead their companies into deceit.

In contrast, the outward evidence of a strong committed character is a consistently high level of conduct despite the circumstances. A commitment to perform high quality work despite inconsistent management styles is a good example of admirable character.

The list of strong character qualities reads like a bi-polar opposite of the individual with weak commitments. Quality work and timely delivery are trademarks of these people. Complete honesty and pure motives mark their personality. There are no slander, revenge motives or alter ulterior plots involved in their conduct. Strong character in an individual not only produces quality work but is also concerned about the individuals impacted by his production.

For example, an outside salesperson has customer service, accounting, finance, clerical staff, management, engineering, and production personnel all depending on their ability to win business in the marketplace. Of course, these individuals must be working as an interdependent team. But each person performs a vital role if the objectives of the company are to be met. The outside salesperson is simply the most visible aspect of the company offering to the customer.

The rewards of strong character are first of all peace and a heartfelt joy that they gave a 100% of their capacity to a quality effort. These people earn trust and respect that turn into sales dollars, raises, promotions, and security. Even if the results do not meet expectations, everyone knows that every effort was taken to have a successful outcome.

These quality efforts often open new doors because of the reliability of the individual bring confidence that new endeavors will be fully explored and vigorously pursued.

Slander

The damage caused by slanderous talk and unchecked gossip falls not only on the individual being reviled, but on the person who is doing the talking as well. If you are unaware of the person's character who is gossiping about another person, the least it can do is to put the victim in question unless you know absolutely to the contrary. If you trust the gossip, then it is extremely difficult to not believe any slander being passed on.

Many people with a habit of gossiping are known to be negative and critical. These people tend to look for the worst in a person or situation. Consequently, these people find the most negative aspects possible and relay their impressions to the first available ear.

This conduct will lead people to lose trust in the slanderous individual and avoid them whenever possible. This costs not only the reputation of the gossip, but the trust necessary for future opportunities and close relationships.

Of course, there are people who will seek out the gossip because they can only feel good about themselves when another person is placed in a negative light. This temptation is very easy to succumb to. Many of us are guilty of listening to untrustworthy information, because it is easier than excusing yourself. And there is something very appealing about having "insider information" or an "informed opinion."

Extreme care must be taken to not think or speak ill of someone unless you have absolute proof to the contrary that their motives and conduct are impure.

Of course, the person who stands to incur the most damage is the object of the slander. The harm done to the reputation and relationships is difficult to calculate precisely. Whatever emotional, physical or financial impact caused is painful and unnecessary.

Political campaigns are very public examples of half-truths being broadcast as absolute truth with the intent to harm. Frequently, inferences are drawn about the opponent that is purely opinion. These conclusions are represented as an intention for the opponent to act in some harmful manner towards the listener.

I remember meeting a man once who impressed me with his friendliness, truthfulness and sincerity. When I made a very positive remark about him to a mutual acquaintance, she proceeded to rip into his character as one of exactly the opposite. Immediately, I began to question his character, because I trusted the woman who made the remarks. The damage had been done, and I never thought of him in the same light again.

These examples clearly illustrate that some parties may have something to gain from their slander and others have experienced hurts that motivate their remarks. Whatever the cause, the hate and lies spread are never warranted by the situation.

The point must be made that information regarding malicious intent toward others clearly does not fall under the category of slander. Overt threats towards toward life, limb and property must be taken seriously. Informing the intended victim and the proper authorities becomes a responsibility, not meddling.

In summary; be sure to put yourself in another's shoes, practice deep concern and consider the consequences of your actions before speaking about another person. Is it true, pure, lovely and praiseworthy? No…then put it out of your mind.

Trust

Perhaps no other word best describes the pre-condition for conducting business than the word trust. The standard question before a purchase has become, "How well do you know this person or company?" Which is another way of asking, "How much do you trust them?" It takes a great deal of effort and consistency to build trust, and it can vanish in a second. If someone has the perception that you are not being straightforward with them, it can damage the trust. But if you are caught in an outright deception, then it can rightfully destroy the trust between the two parties.

The credibility built by delivering exactly what was promised or exceeding that promise builds trust and loyalty. This simple statement opens up Pandora's box when it comes to truthfulness in sales presentations and advertising. Great care must be exercised to present the product and its capabilities in the most truthful light possible. Why has it become so common to see outlandish hyperbole used in advertising products? Does it dawn on the people writing this stuff that no one believes it and it hurts their reputation?

Trust should be treated like an asset that has great value. And in fact, it does. The reason investors pay more than the book value of a company is the impact that trust (called goodwill and other intangible assets) have on the future income of the firm.

Valuing trust means that an organization must closely guard the claims made about its products, the quality of the products, the service oriented around those products, timeliness of deliveries, value of the offering, payments, and the way people are treated. In addition, the accounting and finance functions of the company must be run by the General Accepted Accounting Principles standards and wise cash management. A system of checks and balances should be incorporated that prevent senior management from taking unilateral control of the company's strategies and finances.

As an individual, the factors that allow someone to trust you include truthfulness, consistency, being conscientious, competent, timely, patient, pure, good, kind and forgiving. This type of individual makes an excellent employee, manager or business agent. Contrast these attributes with someone who plays loose with the truth, fails to show up, rarely turns in work on time, delivers shoddy work, angers easily and can't be trusted financially, and then the difference is enormous when dealing with this person.

Early in the 21st century we have witnessed the pain and suffering caused by senior management's deceit regarding the income and profitability of their companies. The Enron case stands out because it had such wide-ranging impact on thousands of loyal employees. Jeff Skilling and Ken Lay were found guilty in May of 2006 of securities fraud, lying to auditors and bank fraud. Skilling was charged with over 40 felony offenses and convicted of at least 32 acts of fraud and lying. Ken Lay was convicted on 10 counts of conspiracy, wire fraud, securities fraud and false statements to banks. The ultimate consequence was the collapse of the company, the loss of thousands of jobs and the failure of the pension fund for the company. The trust that was given to these top executives and other managers in the company was repaid with bitter pain and life changing consequences for the rank and file employees.

Even more heinous are the crimes we see documented in the paper about health professionals and clergy who take advantage of their trusted positions to physically and mentally violate patients and students under their care. This type of misdeed deserves no pardon. These individuals should never be returned to a position of trust with vulnerable people.

At first glance, trust seems to be one of those intangibles that we know when we see it, and we also know when it has been violated. But given a little more thought, these intangibles can be defined clearly and observed in practice. Then, awareness of the principles involved allows us to put them into practice.

A LinkedIn Prospecting Process

Trucon Sales Consulting

www.truconbd.com

The Payoff Benefits

The first benefit is the ability for you to reach out to a massive database and connect with prospects from your target market. You can obtain names, titles, job responsibilities, business bios, e-mail addresses and phone numbers for future contact.

The payoff arrives when your connections reach back out to you to conduct business or at a minimum give you an opportunity to earn their business.

It also provides you with an opportunity to probe into very specific people with the job titles and authority to conduct business with you in the future.

LinkedIn mining saves you prospecting time and narrows your target market. This is a very significant benefit in both the short and long-term life of your business.

Allows you to set up one to ones with prequalified customers and referral partners.

Creates a database for marketing efforts and sales expansion

Step One – An Overview

Revise your profile to look more like a business capabilities website instead of a personal resume.

Include only your name in the name block.

The next lines should be keywords searched by your prospects. Separated by vertical lines.

Example:

Outsourced Sales | Contract Sales | Sales Consulting

Include a professional headshot, not your logo or favorite photograph.

Use all Caps to name your company.

Describe precisely and briefly what you do and then empathize the benefits.

(Example: Business growth stats, money saved due to your applied expertise)

Ask for and post referral narratives for each job listed.

Be sure to include links to your website or specific URL in each job description

Locate and fill in the How to Locate section with phone numbers and your e-mail address.

Look at your Profile strength circle on you profile page and strive to achieve all-star status

Step Two

Join groups in your own market or industry, your ideal client's industry, groups that you are interested in, groups that your target prospects are members of, alumni groups, open groups and some big groups. Once you join a group you can send a message to strategic members /prospects or invite strategic members to connect with you. Search for and join at least 20 Groups with a possibility of the members being business prospects or referral partners.

Step 3

Personalize your LinkedIn public profile URL: Make sure your public profile reflects your name, your business, or your area of expertise: http://linkedin.com/in/linkedinexpert Headers should be; What you do? How you do it? What are the benefits? This is not a personal bio. You must focus on what you deliver to your clients. Work diligently on this rewrite until you are confident that your prospects will be so impressed that they want to call you.

Have a separate website and or blog where individuals can be directed to read more detailed information about your services and capabilities and articles of interest to them. Newsletter articles will be linked back to this website.

Step 4

Utilize the "Experience" description area: Use the 1000 characters in the description section to tell people why they should hire you or your company or buy your product. Put in a testimonial. "Experience" is a great place to list "wins", different companies you have helped, seminars or workshops you have presented, a mini shot of your personal website.

Step 5

It is not absolutely necessary; however you may sign up for the **LinkedIn Premium** services and select **Sales Navigator** as your option

To start your connection process, be aware that you can connect with people in a **manual process** of reviewing people and job titles on a one-by-one basis or you may automate the process for a higher volume of contacts. Linkedin recommends that you add a personal note for each connection request, although it is not necessary.

Using **<u>Chrome</u>** as your search engine tool, buy the professional version of the add on called **Dux-Soup**.

This will allow Navigator (using a defined prospect demographic) and Dux-Soup to look at hundreds of profiles a day on an automatic basis. The goal is for the individuals that you "look at" be curious enough to look at your profile and ask for a connection. Dux-Soup will scan for your titles and geographic preference, then it will generate an excel file for you.

- Note that LinkedIn will be monitoring the number of connection requests and you run the risk of being suspended if you start doing massive amounts of connection requests.

Step 6

Write 10 to 15 "psychological trigger" e-mail messages to be used with new connections and connections that you will add to an automatic e-mail follow up campaign. Do not be overtly aggressive or sales oriented. Include articles your target market audience will want to read about and will encourage them to open your next newsletter.

Trigger e-mails fall in the category of:

1. Consistency – Commitments

2. Authority – Defer to experts

3. Leadership – Inspiration

4. Like – Work w/Likable people

5. Emotion – People make decisions based on feelings more than logic

6. Reciprocity – People repay in kind

7. Social Proof – People follow the lead of others

8. Story – People believe and remember stories

9. Scarcity – People want what they can have less of

Step 7

Ensure that you are posting quotes, videos and links to articles a minimum of 8 times over each 5 day working week into your general LinkedIn account, your groups, Facebook and Twitter.

Step 8

Create a profile of the individual you ideally want to connect with. (See the Navigator parameters – Demographic and Geographic)

Example: VP, CEO, COO of a small to medium size business ($1 mil to $10 mil) in the greater Austin, TX area in the services or software business.

Run a search in Sales Navigator using Dux-Soup to view hundreds of profiles per day. When Dux-Soup stops, export the list into a clearly labeled Excel file for later use.

Step 9

As individuals ask to connect on LinkedIn, decide whether to accept or reject. Marginal connections (considered as only fair prospects or referral partners) should be added to the database and to a monthly newsletter list. Thank them for connecting.

Strong prospects should be entered into the database and be scheduled to receive a LinkedIn messenger e-mail every 5 working days for three weeks. After that time period they can be called or entered into the automatic e-mail program.

Step 10

The automatic e-mail program can be purchased as part of your **Constant Contact** membership (Or another commercially based e-mail/marketing supplier)

Constant Contact allows you to send newsletters and capture opens, to run events and capture RSVP's and with an additional purchase, to have multiple automatic e-mail programs that will send pre-written psychological trigger messages to each individual on a periodic basis. Typically, these e-mails are scheduled every 7 days once an individual is loaded into that specific database. Constant Contact bills based on the size of your database.

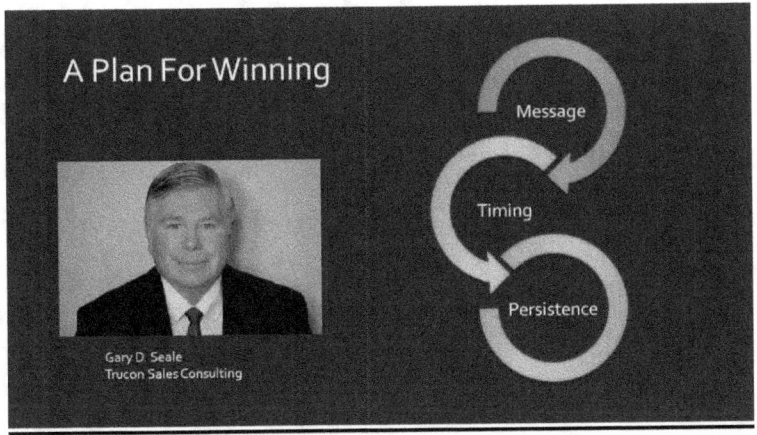

Step 11

Your profile should be monitored for individuals who elect to connect. When they do, they will be sent a simple thank you note and noted in the CRM for regular messaging as noted previously.

Your profile needs be monitored for any correspondence sent to you for a necessary response.

About the Author

Gary D. Seale is an author, sales consultant and speaker who lives in Austin, Texas.

He is an award-winning sales manager and speaker with over forty years of experience in the sales arena with three Fortune 500 companies and several international distributors. For the past decade he has been serving as a sales consultant and sales services provider to multiple clients throughout the United States.

His passion is helping businesspeople achieve their goals through sales management and leadership advice based on his successes in three major industries over his career. This is the second book he has written for entrepreneurs.

Gary D. Seale - MBA

www.ingramcontent.com/pod-product-compliance
Lightning Source LLC
Chambersburg PA
CBHW070537220526
45467CB00003B/966